To reserve your spot...

7LevelSelling...

INCREASE YOUR SALES

7 | LEVEL SALES CHALLENGE

•••

Take your sales career
to the next level with the
7 Level Selling Challenge!

Increase your sales by a minimum
of 15% to 30% in 30 days.

If you don't think that this
information can bring you
at least $1,000,000 or more,
we will refund your money
in full after day 1 of the challenge.

*Conditions apply

•••

To reserve your spot in the challenge go to

7LevelSelling.com/challenge

THE CLOSE

7 LEVEL SELLING

STEFAN AARNIO

Clovercroft Publishing

The Close: 7 Level Selling

©2018 by Stefan Aarnio

Published by Clovercroft Publishing, Franklin, Tennessee

Edited by Tammy Kling and Tiarra Tompkins

Cover Design by Emir Orucevic

Illustrations and Interior Design by Adept Content Solutions

Printed in Canada

ISBN: 978-1-948484-14-5

CONTENTS

THE CLOSE—7 LEVEL SELLING

Stefan Aarnio

I Could Feel It In My Bones

My Journey: How the Commitment to Sales Changed My Life

I could feel it in my bones . . .

When I was a teenager my mother and father always insisted I get a summer job. Mom was a schoolteacher, and my father ran his own business, and they wanted to teach me the important lessons of hard work and life skills.

This endeavor was noble, as I was a young man and needed to learn about money and work, which makes up much of a man's purpose in life. Work is important, and since most people spend 70 percent of their waking hours working, it's critical that you eventually do what brings you fulfillment.

Unfortunately a large majority of people do not like their work.

Looking back, I should have probably encouraged myself to work more throughout the year and even more in the summertime, but the idea around our home was to get a summer job when school was out and then quit and focus on school during the rest of the year. The general idea was to save up money for university tuition because after all, "Go to school, get good grades, and get a job" was the Valhalla, the heaven, the Promised Land for generations of young people since 1930 and a "good job" would solve all of my problems in life. Every year I would get good grades that would one day get me into a good university, and the good university would get me a good job and economic salvation and happiness would be mine!

At least that's the bullshit story sold to young people every day in the public schools.

Years later when I graduated at the ripe young age of twenty-two with a major in English and minor in music, I found that the only work available to me in my home town of Winnipeg, Manitoba, Canada, was a call-center job in the middle of the night, selling luxury hotel rooms to rich people. The job required a degree, and after it was all said and done, being the #2 salesman in the office, I earned a meager $10 an hour which was minimum wage at the time.

The dream I had been sold on getting a good job and great education was completely false, and it was indeed an old, outdated idea, a relic of a time that had passed by the year 2008 when I officially entered the workforce full time. The pain that I felt in my heart from being sold a false dream put me in a post-grad depression, and I had to do some major soul-searching to find the real path to my purpose in life, economic success, and the business of selling!

Every summer as a teenage boy I would sit down at the kitchen table and open the newspaper to the "JOBS" section and "LOOKING FOR HIRE" section in the classifieds. I would pour over the ads trying to find a loophole in the marketplace where I could earn something above minimum wage that would be fun and exciting. I was a young man and craved an adventure.

I had been a line cook one summer, after McDonalds and Walmart rejected me (along with every other local business.) I was a young man, seventeen years old, and relatively unconnected in the world. My parents were modest people: my father ran a T-shirt brokerage he called a business; my mother was a government, unionized, high school teacher.

None of the jobs made sense to me in the paper.

One was $5 an hour, another $6.25 an hour; painting homes was $10 an hour. Little did I know, but my own parents were setting me up for abysmal economic failure in trying to find work that made sense after meeting their unrealistic demands for an acceptable job. They gave me a list of criteria under which I could find work to pay my university bills in the fall. The work I was to find had to be the following:

1. Guaranteed hourly pay—my parents were both left wing socialists who were terrified of commission based jobs and capitalism in general. They claimed that in a commission based environment "you won't make any money" and "the company will screw you out of your commissions. They had a negative view on selling and making money in general.

2. My parents encouraged me to "follow my dreams" which meant go into something with music (my passion at the time that fed my vain delusion to be a rich and famous rock star)—yet there were no music jobs, especially music jobs that were guaranteed hourly pay. There was a small minority of government grant-funded music jobs, but they were typically reserved for women and minorities as per government mandate, and as a young single white male, I was excluded from these positions due to "employment equity" standards. The employment equity standards were there to include everybody, but the very idea that was inclusive to some was discriminating to me.

3. "No selling" was a rule for the jobs I was to take: my father was a failed salesman who was fired from his last sales job in 1988, when I was two

years old, right before my younger brother was born. This pissed my mother off and demoralized my father.

The idea of me taking a career in sales terrified my mother so much because of my father's bad experiences, and the idea of selling left a bad taste around salespeople in my father's mouth. This was ironic because my father was a business owner who should have embraced the idea and profession of selling, but he was a socialist at heart and had limiting beliefs around making and keeping money.

4. "No night shifts" insisted my father! He claimed that night shifts were too dangerous for a young seventeen-year-old boy, and they didn't want me to be mugged or killed in our city of Winnipeg in the middle of the night. Winnipeg was the official murder capital of Canada at the time, and my parents did not want me to be become a murder statistic.

This left me with the lowest paid and most meaningless work available. I was a young man with big dreams in my heart, but I was being treated like a young kid. All that was left was Tim Horton's, the famous donut chain where I had to wear a humiliating hair net to hold my long rock-star hair together. I stood behind a cash register taking coffee orders wearing an emasculating unisex tan uniform that was made of plastic so coffee could not stain the company-owned slacks and golf shirt. This plastic uniform was their property, so the management informed me I would have to give back if I quit. I was fine with giving the uniform back at the end of the summer.

I had always felt a pull to do something different.

At age sixteen I could feel a burning desire in my bones, an intuition to drop out of school and go sell. But I didn't listen to this intuition at the time and instead listened to the artificial advice from my parents. I was a natural-born salesman, negotiator, and closer, but nobody knew it at the time. My talents and skills lay dormant under a thick layer of self-doubt and loathing towards my natural talents in selling. I stayed in school until I was twenty-two, lost my way in life and slipped into a post-grad depression before finding my path in a very rewarding career of professional selling.

The idea of selling to live made sense to me, because both of my grandfathers had been successful entrepreneurs. I just knew that sales, money, and entrepreneurship pumped through my veins. The money made sense to me, the idea made sense to me, and every fiber of my body knew and agreed that selling was right for me. A burning desire coursed through my veins. I knew selling was right, and that it was in my blood, I could feel it in my bones. However, my parents loved me, and they tried to protect me from pain, suffering, and hardship.

I felt like I was being choked out of building any real skills or any real value in the world. This is demoralizing and confusing for a young man.

In the famous words of Ayn Rand, "Man is the only animal that cripples his children's ability to survive." My parents in their smothering love did not understand that the job restrictions they placed on me were crippling my ability to become a useful member of society.

After being hired at age twenty-three for my dream job with a small private equity firm selling shares in large real estate investment deals, I was ecstatic! The elation I felt made me higher than a kite, to finally be doing something I wanted to do with my life. I had been wandering the hot dry desert aimlessly up to this point in my life, and I could feel the vultures circling me overhead waiting for me to give up, drop out of my dreams, and go back to meaningless hourly work at a job I hated. But instead I found an oasis in the desert and this new job in professional selling, that I had always craved, was a long cool refreshing drink of water in an otherwise wasteland desert of opportunity.

Within two weeks of being hired, the company flew me out to Edmonton. I packed all my best clothes and hopped on the plane to head west. I didn't need to pack much because my burning ambition and persistence seemed to push me through every obstacle so far.

Flying across the country on a ticket that I had earned by selling myself into my dream job made me feel invincible. Arriving at the head office was a stunning experience, and everything was new, polished glass and shiny. The girls working the desk were gorgeous, young, attractive, and poised models that men of any age or background would kill to possess. The men in the office were striking as well. They were tall, handsome, and extroverted and dressed to kill. They wore sharp tailored suits, shiny black polished oxford shoes, and crisp starched white shirts. The entire office dripped of sex, which the company bottled and sold as investment advice. The company had a winning formula: Hire young hot female models to work in the office, and the young hot models would attract young aggressive alpha males to work as salesmen. These men were supermen: tall and bright. They were also ideal for the financial industry—smart, hungry, and poor. The culture was vibrant and visceral and they only accepted the best.

I felt as though I had joined a winning team, and it was a team that I wanted to be a part of. The salesmen were polished, both in the way they spoke and the way that they looked. If they were diamonds, I was only rough lump of coal. I couldn't compete with their image or sharp wit and vocabulary.

They sat me down in the boardroom with another young recruit named David who was later nicknamed Buck by some of the alpha males in the office. Buck was also a rough lump of coal with a shaggy haircut that had grown wild around his ears and badly needed trimming. However, underneath his shaggy hair, Buck fit the description: tall, handsome, athletic and smart. With the right polish, Buck would make a great salesman. We sat together in the boardroom until a group of men entered. Two were executives from the company, and barely a few years older than me. These executives were different from the visceral alpha male salesmen. They were more effeminate, polished and nerdy with glasses. The other two men were much older, either in their fifties or sixties.

I quickly learned that the two younger men were here to train me and Buck. They were unbelievably young, but they were executives, so we treated them like the experts. We sat in the boardroom for a full day, learning how to organize and take notes.

To my surprise, that one full day was the entire extent of the training program for the company and although I was in Edmonton for seven days of training, they had no further content to teach me about sales. The two older men who sat with Buck and myself were newly hired by the company as sales consultants and were assigned to us as mentors.

There was very little briefing or introduction to our new mentors, but I quickly learned that these two older men had spent their entire life selling vacuum cleaners door to door. These men were proven warriors in the art of direct sales. They had sharpened and perfected their tools selling every day for their entire adult lives. The moment I learned that my mentors were professional vacuum cleaner salesmen, I began to cringe.

The nagging voice of my mother entered my brain and I felt as though I was in the wrong place. My palms started to sweat and my fingers formed into fists as I felt the urge to stand up and run out the door. I thought I was selling investments, not vacuum cleaners! What did these men know about selling investments? I suddenly felt dirty, but at the same time my life had finally come full circle.

When I was seventeen and looking for a summer job in the newspaper, I had scoured the classifieds and noticed an ad that read, "Make $85 per hour!" My heart jumped the minute I saw that kind of pay and I immediately dialed the number in the ad. A young pretty voice answered the other end of the telephone and she told me to come to the office tomorrow at 10 AM and "dress sharp."

After I hung up the phone I immediately dialed my grandmother to tell her the great news that I had a job interview and that I wanted to borrow her car to drive across town to get the job. I arrived in an industrial part of town full of derelict homes, train tracks and empty warehouses. I quickly located the building where my interview was to be held and parked on a side street. The building was a blank brick industrial bunker with no windows and only one mirrored-glass door on the front. No sign, no markings, completely anonymous. I knocked on the door at 10am for my appointment and no one answered so I went back to grandma's car and waited for ten minutes. I went back to the front door at 10:10 AM and the door pushed open revealing a beautiful reception area. A young handsome man in his late twenties introduced himself to me as "Mr. Ellice." He had a huge, white smile from ear to ear and was dressed in a perfectly tailored and pressed dark navy suit. I felt uneasy about the unmarked building and the fact that no one was there to answer the door at 10 AM, but Mr. Ellice's appearance and demeanor made me feel at ease.

I sat in the lobby and filled out the application forms for the $85 per hour job and surprisingly, there was no one else in the lobby applying for this position. Maybe I was in luck. Finally, Mr. Ellice called me into his office around the corner and I handed him the forms I had filled out. He looked at my résumé and the forms I had spent fifteen minutes filling out and then quickly pushed the papers aside. Instead, we talked about my dreams of being a rock star. After about 15 minutes of banter Mr. Ellice said "I've got three positions available in my company, one is for secretaries, but you don't want that . . . two is my warehouse guys, but you're smarter than that . . . and three are my sales guys. I overpay everyone and I think you would be best suited to sales because you're a great guy to talk to! I want you to call me today at 5:00 PM, and I'll let you know if you got the job."

I felt very excited to have made it this far in the interview process and quickly asked Mr. Ellice what I was going to be selling. He replied, "It's a cleaning product about the size of a football and it's going to change the world!"

Wow, I thought to myself, I'm going to change the world!

I drove back to my grandmother's house and as I returned the keys for her car, I told her that I was going to be selling something: "A cleaning product the size of a football that would change the world!" My eighty-four-year-old grandmother lit up with excitement and as a lady who grew up on a farm, she was always excited when anyone in her family got a new job. My grandmother was also very curious about my pitch and the cleaning products that would change the world. She was so curious and promised to buy whatever I was selling. I was so excited; I already had a sale before I even knew what I would be selling!

I called back Mr. Ellice at 5:00 PM on the nose. He answered the phone and said "Stefan, I'm so glad you called; out of the eighty interviews I did today, you were the one guy I wanted to talk to. Come in tomorrow for training and orientation. It's a three-day, unpaid training, but on Monday morning we'll have you making money right away!"

Then he hung up the phone. I felt as though I had won the lottery. $85 per hour was a lot of money, more than ten times the minimum wage at the time. I didn't think about the fact that it would be impossible to do eighty interviews in one day. I didn't think that I would be the only one calling him back at 5:00 PM, but I didn't care. I felt like I had won the lottery.

The next morning I showed up at the unmarked bunker and was ushered into a back room. Inside the room were five young sales candidates sitting in chairs wanting the same job I did. They were young, good looking, and dressed to kill. Out of the five sales candidates, one was a former Xerox salesman, one was an ex-car salesman, one was a med student, one was a single mother, and the other was a student like me. Mr. Ellice greeted us at 9 AM, and we all waited eagerly to see the product we would be selling, but first, we were introduced to Clancy.

Clancy was the owner of the company, in his mid-forties, with skin that was so tanned that he looked like a baseball glove. He had a pencil-thin mustache and was balding with a bad black greasy comb-over. He wore a yellow dress shirt that was unbuttoned far too low, and he had a beer belly that hung over his belt. I wasn't sure if his beer belly was from drinking beer or just working too hard and living the salesman life. He had multiple gold chains around his neck and far too many gold rings on his fingers. He looked like a wrestling promoter, a low-level pimp or a Mafioso. His black intense eyes fixated on us from behind his horn-rimmed glasses, and he took the stage from Mr. Ellice quietly and intensely.

"Are you guys ready to see what you're going to be selling?" Clancy asked.

"YES!" We cried out in unison; we were all high on the idea of making fast easy money.

"Alright, let me show you." Clancy pointed to a box behind him that was covered with a black sheet the size of a large microwave. Like a magician, he grabbed one end of the black curtain and whipped the curtain like he was pulling a rabbit out of a hat. The excitement peaked, and suddenly, we were all staring at a generic, brown, cardboard box.

The room was silent. We were all looking at this box, but no one could identify what was inside. Mr. Ellice, Clancy's magic show assistant, got down on his knees and opened the box quickly, as if the magic was wearing off of the presentation. Finally he pulled out a shiny, metallic, space age looking machine.

Mr. Ellice held up the machine like a prized fish that he had caught in a fishing championship. We all stared at it, mystified at its beauty, but unable to identify what we were looking at until finally someone said:

"It's a vacuum!"

A vacuum? I thought to myself. I can't sell vacuums! Vacuum cleaner salesmen are slimy and I'm not slimy!

My internal dialogue was outraged. I had driven across town twice and sat through meetings, and now I was being sold on selling vacuums. I knew that everyone in the room wanted to leave the minute we realized that Clancy and Mr. Ellice had tricked us into watching their vacuum presentation, but we were too polite and we were already committed, so no one dared to leave.

Mr. Ellice dazzled us with the unbelievable features and benefits of this space age vacuum. It was a truly impressive machine, built with a mini jet engine inside that would last for forty years. He told us the backstory of the machine and the fact that it was built in a re-tooled jet engine factory from World War II. He told us about the magnesium finish that was nearly indestructible and that it would bounce but not dent if you threw the vacuum across a cement driveway (which Mr. Ellice informed us was one extreme way to close a sale). The hose of the machine was made of neoprene, the same material that they make deep sea diving wet suits out of, and finally, Mr. Ellice dumped fifteen pounds of sand into the vacuum, opened the door, and dumped the sand on his head, but magically, the sand did not fall out. The amazing jet engine flow of air was flowing so strong through the machine that it held the fifteen pounds of sand magically in place when a lesser machine would have the sand dump onto Mr. Ellice's head. When I saw the sand trick, I was sold—I wanted to be a vacuum salesman!

After nearly an hour of watching the magic show, we were all sold on selling vacuums, and Clancy took the stage as things began to get serious:

"How much money do you want for selling one of these things?" Clancy's tone was confrontational and he stared us down like a thug while he slowly walked over to a sales flip chart.

No one said anything. We were too intimidated.

"$600?" Clancy barked. There was no response. The room was silent.

"Six hundred bucks for selling one of these things?" Clancy asked rhetorically as he continued to stare us down. He wrote a big $600 on the flip chart without breaking eye contact with us, and still no one moved.

We had no idea about what was a fair commission to sell a vacuum, but $600 did sound appealing to me. If I only sold one vacuum a week I would be making way more money than my other summer jobs painting houses.

"How about $700?" Clancy wrote $700 in huge numbers on the flip chart and we began to squirm.

$700 sounded even better.

"How about $800?" Clancy wrote a huge $800 on the flip chart and we began to look at each other and began to smile. I couldn't believe it. Selling vacuums suddenly seemed to be the best thing since sliced bread.

"Listen, you guys sell one in a week, I'll pay you $600 a sale. You sell two in a week, I'll pay you $700 per sale, and if you sell three in a week, I'll pay you $800 a sale!" Clancy began to circle the $800 on the flip chart, and I began to grin thinking that I was going to make more money than I ever had in my life by selling vacuums. Suddenly, my enthusiasm for this machine began to swell, and my beliefs about selling vacuums began to instantly change.

I spent the next three days in training and every half day, one of the sales candidates would drop out. We would come back from lunch and there would be one less person in the room. After three days, I was the only one left.

"It's time to do some real live demos." Clancy said at the end of the third day. "If you do six demos, whether you sell or not, I'll give you a hundred and fifty bucks . . . It's not much, but it will help you buy some bread and sandwich meat on Monday morning."

I pictured myself buying a few loaves of rye bread and deli ham to survive the week. Getting into sales was becoming real for me. I could even imagine tasting the ham, rye bread, and yellow hot dog mustard that I had earned by selling.

I had worked for three days for no pay and was beginning to get hungry from not earning any money. The idea of $150 appealed to me greatly, and I knew that it wouldn't be that difficult to show this vacuum to my friends and family. The idea of buying some bread and meat also seemed appealing. I wanted to earn my sustenance for the week instead of living on handouts from mom.

I took one of the vacuums home and called everyone I knew to make my six presentations. My mother fought me every day when I came home from sales training: "Sales is a hard life! Your father always wanted to sell but he didn't make any money! Sales companies always screw you out of commissions!" All along the way my mother relentlessly barraged me with negativity until the third day when I emotionally collapsed.

For those three days I had attended sales training eight hours each day, came home and fought with my mother for several hours, and then slept for eight hours. Life became a grind.

Finally, on Monday I showed up at the office and gave my demo vacuum back with tears in my eyes. I was frustrated and wanted to see if I could make it in sales. "Mr. Ellice, I quit. My mother doesn't support me doing this, and every day when I go home she fights with me. I'm exhausted and I just can't do this . . ."

Mr. Ellice looked me in the eye and said, "That's fine, maybe this isn't for you. Just let me ask you one question. Will your mother stop you from doing other things you want to do in your life?"

"No, I don't think so," I said meekly staring at the floor. I told Mr. Ellice with my words that my mother would never hold me back, but in my heart, I wasn't sure. I returned the vacuum in the same cardboard box I had borrowed it in and left the sales office forever.

Years later when I was assigned my mentor in the sales office in Alberta, I knew I was in the right place in my life. I had wanted to sell vacuums years ago and now I was right where I belonged, back with the vacuum salesmen, earning my bread and ham. Some people believe in fate, I believe that there are certain people in life that you are destined to meet, and sometimes you just don't meet them right away. Somehow, through fate, everyone ends up where they belong. My heart had wanted to sell vacuums years ago, and now my current mentors were vacuum salesmen. Steve Jobs said, "You can only connect the dots looking backwards," and now I could see that there was a bigger reason why my vacuum dreams were put on hold. In the big picture, my place was to sell real estate investments instead of vacuums. I just couldn't see the big picture when I was younger.

There is a cost to your life if you fail to learn to sell!

Love it or hate it, we all sell every day. Some of us have nothing to sell, so we sell our time hourly to our boss at a wholesale rate that is barely above the poverty line for most people. J.O.B. is an acronym that stands for "just over broke" because what your employer is paying you hourly will never pay you what you are worth. Instead he will only pay you enough to keep you "just over broke," enough to keep you working, but not enough to be able to live life on your terms!

Selling is one of the last noble professions that allows for upper class movement in our society. Throughout human history, the only social upward mobility was from the military. You fought wars, won wars and got rich. Today we live in a world where the only real professions that give you a chance at becoming affluent, wealthy or rich are:

1. Straight commission sales
2. Investment banking
3. Business ownership and entrepreneurship

All other professions, I would argue—even law and medicine—have such horrendous taxes and controls on your time to stop you from really earning and becoming affluent, wealthy or rich. You also need loads of student debt and up to ten years in school where you do not produce a dime of money for yourself until you graduate. Ten years of nonearning for a young person can set you back financially because anyone can become a self-made millionaire in five years, so ten years for med school doesn't even really make sense if you are truly driven to succeed economically.

Sadly, most people avoid sales like the plague. Ideas like sales is grimy, sales is unethical, and the worst limiting belief of all "selling is bad" or "money is the root of all evil" keeps more people poor and middle class than I could ever count.

Don't be seduced by the idea that you can live a comfortable life in the middle class in the modern Western world. For the last forty years, the middle class in America, Canada, and every other Western country has been systematically getting financially murdered by inflation, rising housing costs, rising debts, rising taxes, stagnant wages, educational inflation, and a myriad of other financial systems designed to fleece the middle class like sheep shorn for their wool. The middle class dream is dead; it's gone, it's a relic from the 1950s and 1960s in America, and if you want to be middle class these days, you need to move to India, Brazil, China, Mexico, or other up-and-coming nations that are growing their middle classes. If you are going to live in Canada or the USA or any other Western or European nation, you must make the conscious choice and effort to be rich.

First-world countries are defined as having a rich class, middle class, and poor class. Third-world nations only have the rich and poor with no middle class. Canada, the USA, and Europe are slowly becoming third-world nations with the eradication of the middle class, so you must choose which side you are going to be on: rich or poor? The choice is up to you and your daily actions!

All of these negative beliefs around selling and making money that I inherited from my parents were toxic and poisoned my mind, body, and emotions when it came to achieving economic and financial freedom. Friends and family continued to poison me and would continue to poison me to this day with average and middle-class thinking if I would choose to speak to them about my dreams. Sometimes the most negative people in your life have the same last name as you.

In the words of Confucius, "The man who says it cannot be done must not interrupt the man doing it."

These negative beliefs had pointed me towards a life of poverty as a "poor musician," and in 2008 after graduating from the University of Manitoba, this wrong thinking manifested as a poverty situation for myself. In 2008 I was:

1. Effectively broke. I made $1,000 a month teaching guitar out of my mother's living room and had very little cash.

2. I had a useless degree with a major in English and minor in music from the University of Manitoba which virtually opened no new economic doors in life for me. I quickly realized after graduation that I was making more money painting houses in the summertime than I could make with my degree. I viewed this as a major failure in my own decision making and my parents' life advice.

3. My mother told me to get a "real job"; now that I had a degree and I ended up with a $10 an hour call center job in the middle of the night

selling luxury hotel rooms for straight commission—this was not what I imagined I would be doing after graduation. This job required a degree to work there as well.

4. I had a $10,000 a year annual income from teaching guitar lessons in my mother's living room, but had done that side job since I was sixteen; at twenty-two this job was not fulfilling my economic needs of being a young man.

5. I spent most of my time living on my mother's couch in her living room, devouring books, trying to find an answer to my economic problems, which was perilous, especially as I tried to avoid selling and sales.

6. I could not afford a car, so I rode the bus

7. I had no cell phone and relied on my mother's landline, which was embarrassing.

8. I had long hair and a bad self-image: long hair, with a dark trench coat, big black headphones, and big black boots. I was scary looking.

9. I had a failing rock band that was supposed to be my business and life raft towards a chance at economic salvation.

10. Because of my situation, I couldn't get a date with a girl although I wanted a girlfriend badly.

11. I didn't know what a mortgage was or anything about money or finance because they don't teach that in school.

In essence the difference between the rich and the poor is three types of capital:

1. Real capital also known as real money, cash, credit, and investors; this is obvious.

2. Intellectual capital also known as intellectual property and having specialized practical knowledge that will yield higher earnings than the middle class and poor.

3. Social capital also known as a large network of other powerful and useful people from which real economic opportunities come.

I had none of the above at age twenty-two and felt desperate to change my situation. If I had failed to make a change to become a student of professional selling, my life today would be a life of "scraping by" and perpetual poverty.

So what was my turnaround point?

My turnaround point was when I embraced the idea that I must become a professional salesman to reach my economic dreams.

I read a book on my mother's couch in my post-grad depression called Rich Dad Poor Dad by Robert Kioysaki. I owe much of my success to Robert today for opening my eyes to real estate investing, selling, and the virtues of owning a business and being an entrepreneur. This book was like rediscovering rock'n'roll or hearing Jimi Hendrix or Led Zeppelin play for the first time.

The book completely changed my world view on money, business, finance, and selling. I became obsessed with business and investing and shut down my vain musical rock star dreams and traded my instruments, home studio recording gear, and PA system in for seed capital to start a business of my own.

I drove across the country to meet Kioysaki and hear him speak when I was just starting out. I was new, I was weak, and I thought that the Guru Robert Kiyosaki could fix all of my problems with a few words from his magical mouth like Jesus would cure lepers.

Robert Kiyosaki is the #1 personal finance author in the world and has sold over 40,000,000 copies of Rich Dad Poor Dad officially and several million more of pirated copies in circulation.

I stood in line at a convention to meet my guru, my sage, my savior to drink the manna of his wisdom for only a brief moment. As I stood in line to have my book signed, I thought of an intelligent question to ask him at the table. In Kiyosaki's journey, he didn't start to become successful with money until he learned to sell by working at Xerox after serving in the US military in the Vietnam War.

As I approached my guru, my sage, for some advice on what a young man could do to be rich one day, I asked him "Robert where is the best place to learn to sell these days? I know you went to Xerox for the training back in the day, but where would you go today?"

He looked up from his book signing table, unimpressed with my question, then signed my book and looked away. "Anywhere," he muttered as he pushed me along in the line.

"Anywhere . . ."

That was anti-climactic and disappointing advice to me at the time, but Robert was right: You can learn to sell "anywhere." Sales is a lifelong study, and the highest paid people in the world are actors, athletes, and salespeople. You can truly learn to sell—anywhere!

I began to dedicate my time to my profession in sales and studying how to become an effective questioner, presenter and closer.

My life after acquiring a degree of mastery in sales today looks much different than my pre-selling days.

Today as I write this book at age thirty-one, my life is 180 degrees different from age twenty-two.

I give you this list of benefits not to brag, but to show you that if you commit to make a study of sales much like a medical doctor studies medicine over ten years in his life, you will make income in excess of a doctor, lawyer, or any other white-collar professional.

The benefits I enjoy today in my life because of my dedication to the profession of sales:

1. I am the owner and operator of two multi-million dollar companies and continue to start and grow companies all the time.
2. I am a self-made millionaire before the age of thirty.

3. I live in one of the nicest addresses in my city.

4. I am a 7-figure earner at a time when $250,000 is a top 1 percent rate of pay in my country and for my age of thirty, a top 1 percent income earner has only $120,000.

5. I am the author of several books on money, business, and real estate.

6. I have won several awards for investing and entrepreneurship including Rich Dad International Hall of Fame. Rich Dad Education only gives out one award a year in Canada. To give you some perspective, there are more people in Canada with Olympic gold medals than in the Rich Dad Hall of Fame.

7. My real estate students have gone on to win national awards including "investor of the year" from a Canadian real estate wealth magazine.

8. I coach and train several MBA grads, doctors, award winning investors, authors, and other very successful people into becoming more successful even though I do not have an MBA or doctorate of my own.

9. I have enough passive income from my real estate to cover my living expenses and don't have to work but rather choose to work every day because my work is my passion.

10. I do work only that I love.

11. I fly all over the world training others to become successful in real estate and business because I believe it is my purpose.

12. I bill out $1,000 to $2,000 per hour for my time in consulting and have a successful consulting practice.

13. I have a growing client list that grows on autopilot everyday through internet marketing and brings me customers every day for a predictable price per customer.

14. I usually take at least thirty days off at Christmas time to reflect, reset my body, and focus on my life and my health. I can take four vacations a year but get bored sitting on beaches.

15. I can afford to pursue passion projects and things that do not serve my business economically but are things I have always wanted to do (like publishing books unrelated to my business, especially fiction books).

16. I have the goal to publish twenty books in my lifetime; as I write this book, my fourth. I also own all my own intellectual property and publishing rights. This is a major key to getting rich and staying rich as so many people lose their intellectual property and rights over time.

17. I can get dates with beautiful women easily; in fact sometimes I go on too many dates. This is a real change in self-image and confidence from being broke nearly a decade ago.

18. I own and drive a car, but do not care for cars. If I could live in my city without owning a car I would.

19. I have raised millions and millions of dollars for my own real estate deals, have flipped over 100 homes, my company purchases on average a home a week for flipping, holding or wholesaling purposes. These homes are all purchased with none of my own money.

20. I have been solicited three times for a TV show on flipping houses, and have been under option with several production companies. I admittedly have not earned a TV spot yet, but there are several more years left to land an official show.

21. I have other people operating my key businesses so I can do the most important things in life.

22. I have money in the bank and sleep like a baby at night.

23. I have a maid and a personal shopper and do not cook or clean because I don't like to do those things, don't do laundry, or generally any tasks I don't enjoy doing including shoveling snow and mowing lawns. The work is not beneath me, but I understand that it's better to make $1,000 an hour than to do $10 an hour labor.

24. I order whatever I want at restaurants and don't have to check the prices.

25. I have people calling me to invest in my companies and offering me money at decent rates even though I don't need the money and will turn them down. I am considering opening a private equity fund to absorb this money into a new business opportunity.
26. I read fifty-two books a year and write one book per year.
27. I know in my heart "every day in every way I am getting better."
28. Although I am older today than ten years ago, I still fit my suits from when I was younger and thinner, and consider myself healthier today than ten years ago.

All of these benefits or similar benefits of your choosing can be yours if you can commit yourself to becoming a professional in the field of sales. Sales is the highest paid hard work in the world and the lowest paid easy work in the world. If you can commit, train, learn, read, and grow through a career in professional selling, you will enjoy a life beyond your wildest dreams.

The life I am living today could not even have been imagined when I was twenty-two. All I could think about was playing the local venues with my band and maybe moving out of my mother's house one day. When you have a career in professional sales and you train like a professional, you will reach heights that others can only dream of.

Sales and entrepreneurship is living a few years of your life in ways that other people won't, so you can live the rest of your life in ways that other people can't.

I salute you in the pursuit of your highest and greatest self, being self-made!

Respect The Grind,

Stefan Aarnio

Everything in Business and in Life Must Be Sold

Contrary to the old adage, "The product sells itself!"

The truth is, that's a lie. No product sells itself, and if you believe that, you have no business in sales. What's the truth about sales? The truth is that the world is full of competition, and every year your competitor is going to try to make things a bit more difficult for you, to refine their product and services and to sell to your prospects. Your competitors aren't going to let the product sell itself; they're going to create a sophisticated sales plan. And even if you're protesting right now and think that you don't have any competitors—a product can't sell itself.

Everything must be sold at some point and whether you are in business or not, you are selling every day. The mother sells her children on getting up in the morning and getting dressed to go to school, the young man sells the young woman on going on a date with him, and of course, there are agents selling real estate, insurance, financial services and commodities every day all around the world.

Everybody Sells, Whether We Want to Admit It or Not

Selling is about influence. How influential are you?

One of the world's legends, convinced royalty to allow him to embark upon a global journey. He's a legend because he influenced (sold) the queen of Spain on his trip and financing his venture into the new world. He also sold his men on an adventure in which they would perhaps die at sea and never return home to their families. **Christopher Columbus** was not just an explorer, he was a salesman.

Another legendary salesman first sold paper cups back in the days when diners only had glass cups to save money, and then he sold milkshake mixers door to door. He was an excellent visionary and unafraid to sell. This salesman finally sold one of the ultimate American business opportunities—McDonalds, a franchise that literally transformed the industry of fast food as we know it. **Ray Kroc**, the founder of McDonalds, will forever be remembered as a legendary salesman but also a visionary entrepreneur.

Other legends include the following:

George Lucas, who had to sell the idea of a new movie called Star Wars to his producer—who hated the idea—but the producer agreed because he wanted George to make other movies for him. The sale was made, and the producer vastly underfunded him. The original Star Wars was destined for failure, only originally showing at forty theatres in America. It later went on to becoming a multibillion dollar earner and one of the most successful movie and merchandising franchises of all time!

Sales legends come in all ages and nationalities, and before you think it's too late to become a sales success, let's look at another well-known visionary who used his influential sales ability to create a business late in life.

Colonel Sanders had failed at nearly every business he started at until he began selling his famous chicken recipe. The colonel travelled across the country establishing KFC's and selling his chicken recipe well into his seventies and his face is one of the most recognized faces around the world. .

Still not convinced of the need to sell? Even talented rock starts need to be persistent and overcome the "no." Rejection and learning how to overcome it is a part of true selling.

The Beatles had to sell their music to countless record companies before finally landing a record deal. The A&R men of their day (arts and repertoire) said, "I don't like their music, I don't like their sound, and guitar is on its way out." Today the Beatles remain the biggest rock band of all time.

The list goes on and on.

Love It or Hate It, Everybody Has to Sell!

For a long time selling has been viewed as a seedy profession, yet that was before the emergence of a strong and solid entrepreneur workforce. In the past when parents had children they often said, "Go to school to get good grades so you can get a good job as a doctor, lawyer or dentist!" You can insert any type of profession into that sentence; we have all heard it before. But today's world is different. With more entrepreneurs working from home than ever before and the resurgence and creation of new entrepreneurial ventures, MLMs and "mompreneur" type businesses, the one who knows how to sell wins. Great sales people are winners.

In reality, today the highest paid professions in the world are actors, athletes and salespeople. If you're an entrepreneur in any industry, you know you've got to sell in order to make things happen. You can either embrace it or fail. It's not just real estate agents or car salesman that sell anymore it's everyone—when the CIO must sell to the board or the CEO; it's actors, it's athletes, and of course it's people with the title of salespeople as well who all sell every day.

So if selling is the highest paid profession in the world, then why don't parents encourage their children to become salespeople?

There are several reasons:

1. **Sales is a profession that demands professional skills, yet is filled with amateurs.** Where a doctor will go to college or university for ten years and spend $250,000 on his education to make $250,000 as a professional, most sales people do not do any training in addition to the mandatory company training at the beginning of their career. In effect, most salespeople do not get the professional incomes that doctors and lawyers get because they don't train like doctors and lawyers. Assuredly, salespeople who train to become the top 1 percent of their field, make

outstanding incomes that are much, much more than doctors or lawyers and are indeed the highest earning professionals in the world.

2. **Sales is a profession with no barrier to entry:** There are no professional papers required to operate as a salesperson; it is not a government-protected profession like a lawyer or doctor, and thus, the profession is filled with people who typically didn't fit into the status quo. The good side to having a low barrier to entry is that selling is "the great economic equalizer" and one of the only professions left on the planet where one can achieve upward social and economic mobility. Countless people throughout history have climbed their way out of poverty and the middle class to achieve financial freedom and great riches by virtue of selling. If you are born poor in sales, it's not your fault, but if you die poor in sales, it is your fault! No other profession has unlimited earning potential and a lack of a "glass ceiling" like selling. The profession of selling is a true meritocracy where merit rules. If you have the skills and the results, you are the golden goose who lays the eggs, and you call the shots in business and in life.

3. **Sales is the highest paid hard work and lowest paid easy work in the world:** Too many people fear the idea of working on commission, when in reality, we all work on commission. If you have a job sweeping floors at the supermarket, you are being paid 100 percent of your wage to sweep 100 percent of the floor. If you only sweep 50 percent the floor, you will be fired and will earn 0 percent of the pay. Sales works the same way; if you only do 50 percent of the work required, you will make $0 in commissions and will eventually be fired by the company, or you will be forced to fire yourself and get another job (perhaps sweeping floors). Sales is a profession where you can put in 95 percent of the work and earn 0 percent of the money. In sales you must put in 100 percent of the work to get 100 percent of the money. In many ways, sales is the most

honest profession on the face of the planet because you make exactly what you produce, nothing more, and nothing less.

4. **A few bad apples spoil the barrel:**—Every now and then you hear of a sales organization that has bad ethics, no ethics, immoral activities, high pressure tactics, failure to pay out sales commissions to salespeople, and overall general fly-by-night business activities. Unfortunately, a few bad sales organizations have spoiled the reputation of the entire sales industry. Most companies that operate in the field of sales (which is all of them) are generally well-behaved corporate citizens, and the ones that operate badly towards their customers or employees go out of business and are replaced by better organizations.

5. **Sales is a humble and honorable profession:** Too many people have a negative idea of knocking on doors, ringing phones, and asking for money. It is visceral and humble to call on people, and often the fear of rejection, fear of criticism, and the fear of failure is too much for most people to bear, which scares them right out of the profession. On the good side, sales is one of the fastest ways to develop yourself as a person and learn to be comfortable with being uncomfortable. Everything you want is on the other side of fear, so I encourage you become great at something you are doing anyways when communicating and persuading the people in your life—which is sales!

Don't forget that many greats have come before you, and even those famous people didn't have a clue what they would become before they became famous. But it all began with the ability to sell. Let's look at a few examples of why you want to work hard today to overcome subtle fears and subconscious self-limiting beliefs.

Arnold Schwarzenegger had to sell his way into the movie business. First they said "your accent will never work" and yet Arnold overcame that and made his Austrian accent a trademark. Then they said the

"Schwarzenegger" name will never work; no one can remember it. Today Arnold Schwarzenegger is one of the most successful actors of all time, and the Apple iPhone even has an autocorrect function to properly spell "Schwarzenegger" so that no one will ever forget his legendary name.

If you've got a limiting belief that you're not good looking enough, don't have the right name, or will never make it in a market that doesn't understand you, it's time to examine and then dismantle those beliefs. The only thing standing in the way is yourself. Another example of someone who overcame the odds and external criticism and limiting beliefs is Oprah.

Oprah Winfrey was told she would never make it on TV, yet she sold herself into a job working at a radio station in Chicago and later sold herself into her own talk show! Not only was she one of the first African American women to dominate the talk show scene, she became a mega brand, known for her first name alone—"Oprah"—and she is also one of the richest women in the world.

Selling is about influence, and persistence. Even horrible humans have used influence as a tool to manipulate the masses. When you learn to sell after reading this book, this will be your greatest challenge. Will you use your newfound sales superpowers for good, or evil?

Adolf Hitler used his for evil and sold his country, Germany, likely one of the most sophisticated countries on the planet at the time, into a brutal three-front war for world domination. He also sold his people into following his views down the path of annihilation, genocide, destruction of the Jewish culture, concentration camps, and other atrocities.

Joseph Stalin sold his country, Russia, a brutal communist regime with millions of his own people imprisoned or killed at the hands of the state. This regime was sold so well that it lasted decades even after he died.

Jesus Christ sold the dominant religion in the western world for the last 2,000 years, and his book "the Bible," means "book" in Greek, indicating that he had the only book to be read for nearly 2,000 years.

The One and Only Way to Make Money in This World

There is only one way to make money in this world, and that is to SELL! You can be a highly skilled accountant, but you'll be a poor one if no one knows that's what you do. Again, it all comes down to selling.

You have two options when it comes to selling. The first is to sell your time, which you may already be doing. Most people sell their time for $10, $20, $30 or $50 an hour. If you are selling time, you will always be limited in your earnings because you are selling a finite resource—your time! We all are equal in time and only have twenty-four hours in a day. You have to sleep a minimum of six hours, so you have eighteen hours left to sell. If you are selling time, you will always be limited when it comes to money.

The other option when it comes to selling is to sell "something else" which may be a product, a service, in the case of real estate it may be a space, a lease, a property. Most people wish to sell something else and wish to have passive income that comes in every month whether or not they are working, but they hold themselves back by failing to master the art of selling.

The Self-Made Path to Getting Rich

Every self-made person who has ever become rich (and stayed rich) in history has followed the same process:

1. **Phase 1—They got a job, (any job will do)**—One of the problems people have starting out is that they have literally no money. Getting a job anywhere, even at minimum wage will solve this first problem.

2. **Phase 2—They entered professional selling and became a master of the art and science**—Once you have a job and an hourly income, the next step is to enter the world of professional selling. I encourage you to get into sales and when choosing an opportunity, typically, the more difficult it is to sell, the better. Commission is better than salary

and you want something that can allow you to become a top 1 percent income earner in society. Once you find a profession in selling, you must stay at that profession until you become a top 1 percent income earner.

3. **Phase 3—The third phase of getting rich usually ends up with starting your own business** and because you learned to sell as a professional, your company grows every year and revenues are strong. People who skip learning the art of professional selling and go to phase 3 usually end up anemic and struggle to make the sales required to stay in business or grow a business. Ninety percent of new businesses fail in the first five years, and 90 percent of the survivors fail in the second five years. If you are a top 1 percent salesperson who starts his own business, you have a much higher chance of success than anyone else because you know how to put cash in the bank!

4. **Phase 4—Sell your business for cash, become a professional investor, and live off your returns.** If you decide to sell your business one day and retire, this is the last phase of getting rich. At this point, usually most people enjoy their business and are passionate about what they do, but if you choose to sell your business and move on to pure investing, congratulations: you have won the game!

INTRODUCTION

Too many people try to start their own business without committing and practicing in the world of professional sales. If you are reading this book, there is a strong chance that you are considering becoming someone who operates in sales as a professional, and I salute you in your pursuit of greatness.

Why Do We NEED Selling More than Ever Before?

The world is changing at a faster pace today than ever before, and what this means is that companies, products, and services are coming into the market faster than ever, and they are also leaving the market faster than ever. The companies that can't survive failed to sell enough to stay relevant, and the new companies coming into the market must sell to survive. Companies today need less people to operate due to technology and many companies have an "everybody sells" policy.

The Merging of Sales, Service, and Brand Experience

With the proliferation of e-commerce and people buying online, the world is becoming more competitive. Competition is good for you because it means there is money to compete for. The new trends in the world of selling are seeing sales, customer service, and brand experience merge into one role. For example, at the Apple store, the sales people there provide service, sales, and brand experience. The same goes for Best Buy: when the "geek squad" comes out to your house to service your electronics, they are also there to enhance the brand experience and make further sales.

The markets of the future will belong to the companies that sell by giving the strongest service and the strongest brand experience, and by virtue of service and experience they will become the champions in their market when it comes to sales.

Sales is too competitive today to be a transaction-focused activity; that may have worked in the 1970s when one company could buy up all of the TV ad space or radio ad space and dominate. Today and into the future, service reigns supreme, and customers are looking for experiences that cannot be commoditized by giant companies like Amazon.

Even companies like Disney are severing themselves from Netflix to control the customer experience. Disney has been a champion of sales, service, and experience and has recently lost ground to Netflix. Disney is smart enough to take back lost ground through opening their own online media portal to compete head to head with Netflix.

Selling has changed throughout the ages and will continue to change into the future. We have gone from a time where the sellers had all the power and we lived in a "buyer beware" society to now living in a "seller beware" society where the buyers of products and services have more power due to the internet and social media.

Selling Will Likely Become One of the Last Professions to Be Replaced by Machines

Due to the complexity of tone, body language, the words to use and the "human touch," selling will be one of the last professions to be replaced by machines (if ever). We live in an age where the "noncreative" jobs such as flipping burgers and driving cabs are quickly being replaced by robots. I don't believe that selling will ever become nonhuman. Why? A great relationship is an asset, and people will do business with people they like, trust, can talk to, and have a bite to eat with. You can't do that with a robot. There are a lot of great ways and methods to automate sales, but the sales role itself is the greatest job security you can have. Why?

Selling, I believe, is the strongest job security you can ever have because of the infinite complexity of human interaction and the fact that most people buy with their "gut" and still want the promise, delivery, and relationship of a real live human. The day when robots or artificial intelligences can make the prospect smile and change their thinking, their heart flutter, and perform complex and long cycle multi touch sales, is the day when every job ceases to exist. If you are a professional in selling, you have job security for life.

The Philosophy of Selling
Selling—Art or Science? Mechanics vs. Delivery

When was the last time you read a book or watched a video on sales?

There are several books, courses, tapes, audios, classes and seminars on selling and rightfully so. Selling is the oldest and most lucrative profession in the world and the only way to make money in this life is to sell something.

Some of these sales resources focus on the mechanics of the sale such as right words, scripts, ratios, percentages and numbers. Other resources rely on delivery, energy, enthusiasm, tone, neurolinguistic programming (NLP), and generally sounding great. Typically extroverted or natural salespeople will rely too much on their delivery, energy and enthusiasm to sell while neglecting mechanics—this is less than ideal!

On the flip side, introverted salespeople will rely too much on mechanics and will miss the humanity behind the sale such as the delivery, the energy and enthusiasm. Selling is both an art and a science and the strongest salespeople develop themselves into becoming ambiverts (right in the middle of introverted and extroverted).

The top 1 percent salesperson will have strong mechanics and strong delivery and will continually hone their craft by focusing on both the art and the science where most average salespeople will rely on one half of the equation.

The Ethics of Selling

The base of a career in professional selling lies in having clean ethics. In short, clean ethics in selling can be summed up as "always do what is right for the customer." If you do what is right, and what is sustainable, you will afford yourself a long and profitable career in the highest paid profession in the world. If you violate your ethics and do what is right for you, but not right for the customer, your sales career and perhaps the lifespan of your company or brand will be cut painfully short. Sometimes doing what's right means you have to do what's wrong for you.

Companies like Zappos who sell shoes online will refer a prospect to a competitor if they cannot offer the right shoe to their customer. The goodwill earned by doing what is right has made Zappos an incredibly strong brand.

Zappos and several other companies have offered "Pay to Quit" programs for years! Amazon borrowed it from Zappos and offered fulfillment-center employees one-time payments to leave Amazon. Every employee gets the offer once a year. The first time, it's for $2,000. The offer increases by $1,000 each year after that up to a maximum of $5,000.

Zappos started it as part of their new recruit program, in order to weed out the short-term thinkers who would take the easy money over hard work, and a commitment to the culture. What a great way to determine whether a team member is going to be the right fit for a company culture and to cement bonding, and long term engagement. By implementing this type of internal program, the company leaders are selling a unique experience and culture. The message? Each and every individual employee eventually gets to face their own personal decision and determine—is this department truly a place I want to be? Do I value this culture and my team members enough to resist the temporary short term gain?

What a great way to show who you are and your commitment to ethics and standards as a leader.

Several companies violate their ethics, which in turn poisons their brand and those unscrupulous companies are forced to "rebrand" their company or simply go out of business. Your personal brand and your company brand take a lifetime to build and can be destroyed in five minutes. To paraphrase Warren Buffet, the world's richest investor, "When you think of things in those terms, you will make decisions differently."

Never sell the customer something he does not need or cannot use is the first rule of ethics. Once you learn the powerful techniques in this book, you will become a master influencer and the dark side of influence can be called manipulation. You will be able to push people to do things that they should not do and so. "With great power comes great responsibility" (Uncle Ben from Spiderman).

Never lie also known as always tell the truth is the second rule of ethics. In selling, you must always tell the truth. This principle holds strong in both business and personal life. The beauty of always telling the truth is that you never have to remember anything. Too many salespeople get lazy in their product knowledge or in their presentation and start telling small lies at first out of convenience that later turn into big lies that can be fatal to the company. If you make a commitment to always telling the truth, you will sleep better at night and stay in business for a long time.

Even if the truth is uncomfortable or you make a mistake, be upfront with people; they will appreciate your honesty, and you will maintain your relationship. A word of caution: avoid the phrase "let me be honest with you," for it implies that everything you said previous to the statement was dishonest. Instead offer to "be upfront" and get all of the issues out on the table. People appreciate it when you are upfront and tell the truth, no matter how uncomfortable the truth is. As a salesperson you will be compelled to tell the good sides about your product or service and downplay the downside of your product.

A smart customer will ask about the downside, and it's your job to be upfront. Your job is to ethically sell for your company while also avoiding "unselling" for your company at the same time. It's okay to focus on the positive side of your product or service because a real customer will likely bring up the negatives before the sale is made. Stay positive and avoid unselling.

Never force someone into buying when it's clear that he should not. We live in a world today where it is no longer "buyer beware"; instead the world has become "seller beware," and consumers and customers in most industries have all of the power.

The power has shifted in the new millennium to buyers having the power with the proliferation of the internet and social media. If you force someone into a sale, they will just as likely cancel on you, complain and wage war on your brand through the internet and social media. Your brand is your #1 asset in this new world, and the only thing that separates you from a low profit is a commodity like coffee or sugar. The market is constantly forcing great products and services down to commodity status, and your brand is what protects the profit for you in your company. If you destroy the brand, you can never get it back.

There are no morals or ethics in *negotiation* but in selling, the customer, when negotiating for price and terms will lie, cheat, and steal to get what he wants. This is clear in human nature and in my book The Ten Commandments of Negotiation. I state that in negotiation there are no ethics or morals; people simply do whatever it takes to get what they want. Your customer may lie to you with the first objection out of his mouth, usually a smokescreen for the real objection. And he lies about his financial situation and lies about needing to "speak to his wife." This is okay for him because we understand and embrace his human nature. On the other side of the table, you, representing your company, brand, product, and service have to operate with the cleanest ethics possible to stay in business indefinitely. Yes it is unfair; the customer will play dirty, and you play clean, but playing clean will be the only way to stay in business indefinitely.

Stop selling, start serving (seller beware) CARING vs. HARDNESS

"They don't care about how much you know until they know how much you care" (Zig Ziglar).

With all of this being said about ethics and doing what is right, I am a believer in the hard close. To define, a "hard close" is close the sale, also known as ask for the money and feel the situation turn from soft to hard, also known as: uncomfortable. Experienced salespeople, natural closers, and great negotiators can sit through a hard close and come out on the other side. I recently bought a property at a steep discount that was worth $230,000, but the vendor wanted $170,000 for the house. I offered $110,000 and the vendor held firm at $125,000. The "hard close" took three hours, the seller kicked me out of his house three times, and he left once, but after three hours we closed the deal at $125,000. I was able to sit through the hardness of the close because I knew that his selling the property to me was right for him and that I was the right buyer. I was justified to sit through the discomfort because of a strong feeling of service and caring for him and because of this justified feeling I was able to reach the reward on the other side.

In contrast, most amateur salespeople will deploy only dead end soft closes such as "so what do you think?" which is likely the worst soft close of all time. They are afraid of getting into a hard conversation with the customer or breaking rapport. This is a mistake and will only yield in fewer sales closed and less revenue for you and your company.

The key with closing hard is to stop selling and start serving. If you are approaching your customer from a strong service standpoint and offering truly the right service and massive amounts of genuine caring for his wellbeing, you can close incredibly hard in an ethical way. However, your hard close can never outpace your level of caring. If you do not care about him enough, you have not earned the right to be hard. Too many amateur salespeople try to get hard without showing a deep caring and appreciation for their customer first. These sales agents are labelled as "pushy salespeople" or "high pressure tactics." These companies will not last in the modern world, and the internet and social media will destroy them almost instantly. If you can show them how much you care and truly mean it, you have earned the right to close as hard as required. In the past, some of my customers have broken out in tears in a hard close, I've even had a customer divorce his wife because she was holding him back. These customers thank me after the sale is made because I cared and stuck it out through the hard moments.

Remember: Your success in life is directly correlated to your ability to have hard conversations. The better you are at lasting and persisting through hard conversations, the more successful you will be in business and in life.

PART ONE

THE OPENING—
THE LANGUAGE OF SELLING

I.

What Is a Sale?

A sale is a transfer of feeling from one person to another and it also is a relationship. We live in a relational world where no matter how much technology gets in the way, human relationships will always remain to be one of the core human needs. To have relationships is to have a rich life and to have no relationships is to live a poor life.

Tony Robbins defines the six human needs as:

1. Certainty
2. Uncertainty or Variety
3. Significance
4. Love and Connection
5. Growth
6. Contribution

A great salesperson will make his prospect feel four of the six needs being: certainty, uncertainty (or variety), significance, and love and connection.

Most people do not buy on logic although they may claim to. Instead, they buy on emotion: "How did this make them feel?" Even large corporations will make decisions based on the gut feeling of a few decision makers and that is why human decision making is usually irrational.

What Is the Basis of All Human Relationships?

The answer is agreement. Anyone you have ever had a relationship with in your life shared a high level of agreement with you, and if there was a disagreement somewhere, that's likely where the relationship stopped developing. If you enter enough disagreement or become disagreeable enough you might get divorced, have a business partners split up, or friendships collapse.

To create an accelerated relationship with your prospect, you must always agree with whatever he says, no matter how nonsensical. In improv acting they call this the "yes and" technique, and it's your job to create agreement with the prospect and never break it. If you and the prospect break agreement, the relationship will break down, rapport will break down, and your chances of a sale will go to zero. Throughout the entire sales process, the most skilled salespeople only get "yesses" out of their prospects and never a "no"

CHALLENGE: When selling aim to get all yesses throughout all parts of the presentation, the opening, the presentation and the close. If you can stay in agreement the whole time, you are very likely to win the sale.

Words to eliminate from your vocabulary: No, But, However. These words create disagreement, create the "no" feeling, and can start an argument. Replace these words with "Yes and"

As a salesperson you will always be making additions and deletions to your vocabulary, and we want to eliminate weak words like "basically," and introduce glamour words like "Tremendous" or power words like "explosive" and "powerful."

What words can you use in your own sales negotiations and process? Take a moment to think and write down five powerful words you'd like to start using today.

The Power of Words

In his book Messages in Water, Dr. Masaru Emoto conducted experiments with words and how they affect water under a microscope. He conducted vast experiments with words spoken to water, written on papers taped to jars of water, and played music to water and observed the effects under a microscope.

What Dr. Emoto found through his research was that words had a profound effect on water and the energy behind the words of "love," "thank you" and other positive emotions formed the water into beautiful crystalline shapes. Whereas negative words or phrases like "I hate you" or "I'm going to kill you" create cancerous looking amorphous blobs that reflect the negative energy behind words.

This has a profound effect on the human body, considering humans are made up of 70 percent water or more. It also explains the power of choosing the right words and more important emotions behind the words to create a pleasing relationship between two people in selling or any other situation. Whether you believe that or not, we can all agree that words are powerful and drive success. If you become a master of words you elevate your chances of becoming successful.

The Language of Agreement

Human relationships are founded on agreement, and the brain has built-in mechanics of letting someone get close or intimate to them. If you follow this wiring and circuitry you can create a relationship with someone at a rapid pace in a matter of sixty seconds or less. All of the switches are flipped on in the mind that says "this person gets me, he understands me." When you are in agreement, your internal narratives will be working together rather than the prospect's internal narrative resisting you and disagreeing silently.

In the words of the famous poet John Donne:

"No man is an island."

Whether you are a new-born baby or the president of the United States, we all rely on relationships and our networks for our basic survival and our ability to thrive.

For those of us who are pursuing entrepreneurship, business, or real estate investing, our relationships are our one and only asset.

We all hear the guru's say, "Your network equals your net worth," but how do we build, grow and maintain a rich network of people?

The most successful people in society are the ones who can establish, build and maintain a large number of significant, intimate, relationships.

But how do we connect on a significant level?

Most people are fairly adept at establishing relationships with people who are similar to themselves. They can find similar interests and form "intimacy" and bonds with people who are *the same* as them over time.

However, most people do not understand the rudiments of establishing a relationship. Further, most people do not know how to master intimacy and bring people closer to them quicker.

Mastering the core 7 levels of agreement can make or break you when meeting someone COLD and you know nothing about them. Many of us are talented at working with WARM meetings, but COLD meetings have higher requirements for establishing connection.

I am naturally a "people person" and can connect very easily with people. However, it's not enough to know HOW to connect . . . we must understand WHY we connect and HOW connection is established.

7 Core Levels Of Human Agreement: "Clichés" to "Needs"

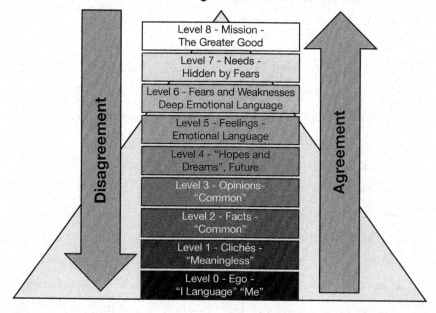

The seven levels of agreement work in a sequence. You cannot jump to the next level of agreement without succeeding on the previous level.

For example, real natural conversations flow through the levels of intimacy in sequence from level 1 to level 7 and they do not deviate from this rule. It's very hard to jump to the "next level" without satisfying the previous level. Furthermore, if you create a disagreement and blockage at a level, you will not advance into the higher levels until you remove the blockage.

These levels need to flow and creating conflict at one level will stop the sequence of connecting.

For illustration purposes, I will artificially construct a conversation between two hypothetical people that could accelerate from level 1–7 in less than three minutes:

1. **LEVEL 1: Clichés**—ME: "hey, how are you?" YOU: "I'm good!"

2. **LEVEL 2: Facts**—ME: "Did you get caught in the rain today?" YOU: "Yes I did, I can't believe the amount of rain outside!!"

3. **LEVEL 3: Opinions**—ME: "What do you think about the Winnipeg Jets coming back to town?" YOU: "I think it's great for the city, it really helps put us on the map."

4. **LEVEL 4: Hopes and Dreams**—ME: "It sure does put us on the map! Why were you running around in the rain today? What would you rather be doing?" YOU: "Ugh, I was running around in the rain because I'm making deliveries for my office, I'd rather be travelling!"

5. **LEVEL 5: Feelings**—ME: "How would you feel if you didn't have to run around in the rain anymore and could travel the world in the way you want?" . . . YOU "I would absolutely love that. Nothing excites me more than travelling."

6. **LEVEL 6: Fears/Weaknesses**—ME "What is stopping you from pursuing your dream? What's holding you back?" YOU "I have a family; I can't put my dream selfishly before them. I need to support them and pay the mortgage. "

7. **LEVEL 7: Needs**—ME "Hmmm . . . What would your family need to survive so that you can pursue your dream and everyone remains happy?" YOU "Well . . . etc."

No matter where you are in the conversation you want to know which level you are on and how to transition up to the next level using a transition question.

NOTE: *If you are selling or negotiating, you cannot "close" until you are on level 7.*

Everyone has needs, and if you can find another person's needs, you can truly help them and create life lasting bonds and relationships.

The majority of the population are preprogrammed to be socially guarded and will conceal weaknesses and needs until you have successfully moved through levels 1–5. This is why prospects lie when retail sales people say "Can I help you?" (Level 7, let me fill your needs) and instead should say "Hey! (level 1 cliché) Have you been here before? (Level 2 Fact). The retail salesperson hasn't earned the right to ask a level 6 or 7 question about needs and things that prospect's problems, so they deflect the communication and send you back to level 0.

In general, levels 1–3 are easy to create an agreement on, but getting to level four (hopes and dreams) is where the rubber hits the road for most salespeople. This is where you want to have your stock transition questions ready to go as well as a well-thought-out script and presentation to navigate the levels and agreement.

Once you create agreement on Level four (hopes and dreams) and transition up to level 5, an emotional connection starts to form, and that is where the sale can start to happen.

Many newbie networkers, salespeople, or negotiators will ask right off the bat, "What are your needs, what do you need?" I especially see this in the network marketing community when I get pitched by new network marketers. The response to these dead end questions is, "I'm fine, go away" (level 0 ego)

Trying to connect on level 7 without building rapport, connection or intimacy through levels 1–6 is nearly impossible. You will get concealment of facts and lies about levels 6 and 7 until you have established a proper base connection.

At best, your prospect will feed you a lie to deflect your inquiry about their higher level needs and will likely say: "I'm fine; I really don't need anything."

How often do salespeople all over the country hear that on a daily basis?

Everyone needs something, including your prospect, and we are all looking for things, and we all have needs all of the time, but the question is, what does the prospect in front of you need? Understanding and identifying this is critical. Can you make a true connection? Can you make a client feel as if you are a trusted advisor instead of a salesperson?

"Hey! (level 1 cliché) Have you been here before? (Level 2 Fact). The retail salesperson hasn't earned the right to ask a level 6 or 7 question about needs and things that are prospect's problems, so they deflect the communication and send you back to level 0.

The 7 Levels of Agreement come from a counselling background where counsellors would have to peel back layers and layers of emotional armor and protection to get to the core needs of a client. As human beings we protect ourselves from exposing weakness and by using the 7 levels of agreement, you can counsel or "coun-sell" your way into the heart of the matter. Only from the heart of the matter can you find understanding and reach a true agreement or make a sale.

Connection happens when you are able to navigate the conversation through levels 1–7 in the proper sequence. You might be in real estate sales and through following this sequence, you may discover that, for example, "their father just died and they're feeling vulnerable. They are the executor of father's house and don't know who to talk to anyone about real estate right now. They are looking for an expert. They don't like realtors and need to sell immediately but are afraid of contracts, contractors, salespeople, and commissions. They also don't want to pay for repairs."

Opportunities come from connecting and being intimate with the people we come into contact with.

All people, rich or poor want one thing: we all want to connect. If you can connect with a person, and move them through the levels of agreement without creating conflict or blockage in the sequence, you will find: what motivates them, what scares them, what their concerns are and finally what they *need* to feel secure to work with you and your company.

The 7 levels of agreement has identified a brilliant pattern in social behavior and has cracked the mechanical code for human connection. If you can memorize or learn a few key questions to "move through the levels," then you will never be stuck in a conversation with nothing to say ever again. You will never be stagnant and will be a master of connection.

The 7 Levels of Agreement Explained and How to Transition Upwards with Stock Questions

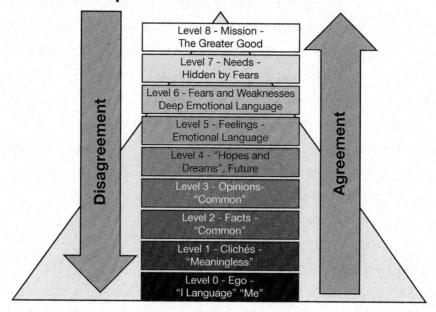

Level 0—Ego

The lowest level of human communication is that of the ego. Speaking from a place of ego will always eventually break connection with your prospect and can potentially harm all the relationships in your life. People who speak at Level 0 are usually in victim mode or survivor mode and have little to say that is relevant to other people because they are self-absorbed. People do not care about you; they care about themselves. As a salesperson you want to ask them about themselves and not about yourself.

You will find yourself in the language of the ego when you say words like:

1. I
2. Me

Talking about yourself in an "I, I, I" way will turn off a prospect faster than a light switch; the same works for "me, me, me" when what the prospect wants to hear is "You" (also known as them). If you are in a sales rut, or are getting negative, or are in victim mode, the quickest way out is to practice gratitude for the things you have—write them down: "I love my life," "I love my family," "I love my job" (even if you don't). By telling yourself you "love" (a form of gratitude) it will rewire your brain out of negativity, into positivity, and out of the ego.

If you meet a prospect who can't get out of Level 0 ego, victim mode, you must do your best to bring him up through the levels of agreement to connect with him and create connection by feeding his ego. "As an expert yourself Bob, you would know." Play him up, make him feel like the boss, and agree with his ego.

Level 1—Cliché

Clichés are defined by Google as:

cli·ché

klēˈSHā/

noun

noun: **cliché**; plural noun: **clichés**; noun: **cliche**; plural noun: **cliches**

1.   a phrase or opinion that is overused and betrays a lack of original thought.
"the old cliché "one man's meat is another man's poison.""

synonyms: platitude, hackneyed phrase, commonplace, banality, old
saying, maxim, truism, stock phrase, trite phrase;
old chestnut
"a good speechwriter will steer clear of clichés"
• a very predictable or unoriginal thing or person.
"each building is a mishmash of tired clichés"

but in a nutshell, a cliché is something so common that it's meaningless. Everyday people have meaningless conversation with others on the cliché level "What's up?" "Hey," or "How are you?" (without really caring).

Any basic human being can create agreement with a cliché and we are so used to it we don't even think of it:

"Hey!"

Response: "Oh hi, how are you?"

Oftentimes once you are engaged in a conversation, you blew past level one seconds ago, and it didn't even register with your brain. That's how meaningless a cliché is, so common it's meaningless.

Note: Intergenerational clichés don't mix. Saying "Wassup?" to a ninety-year-old WWII veteran will not go over so well, just as much as if the war vet gave you slang from the 1930s. It's best to avoid slang at all costs. People who do not speak English as their first language will also have trouble with street clichés too, just as much as they have slang words in their language that are untranslatable, meaningless, clichés. Move out of clichés as fast as possible.

1. **Cliché Transitioning Questions**
    o Hey!
    o Hello.
    o What's up?
    o How are you?
    o What have you been up to lately?

Level 2—Facts

Once you have agreed on clichés you will naturally move onto facts. Facts are typically unemotional statistics that are barely more meaningful than clichés.

25 percent of the population wants to be right over all other things, typically people in the professions of engineering, law, medicine and science. They will debate you over the most mundane facts, so it's best to create agreement and move on.

2. **Facts Transitioning Question**
    o Nonpersonal
        •   What was the score of the game?
        •   What is the weather forecast?
    o Personal
        •   What did you do today?
        •   What have you learned recently?
        •   What have you been reading lately?
        •   What is your favorite color, food, song etc.?
    o Business
        •   How did you hear about us?
        •   What made you contact us?
        •   Did you receive your service as promised?
        •   Did you order the product I suggested?
        •   Who did you bring with you to the event?

Level 3 Opinions

Opinions is where most poor conversationalists fall apart. Opinions can be light or they can be heavy. As long as you typically stay away from the heavy belief system threatening ones like religion, sex, politics, and money, you should be able to navigate through this section easily.

Here is where you can start asking some questions about what the client thought about the product they received in the past—what they like, what they don't like. Typically you want to ask open ended questions that follow the WWWWWH pattern (who, what, where, when, why, and how).

It's important in keeping the agreement that you only ask questions that they know the answer to in level 3; otherwise, you will put them into a state of weakness that will break the rapport. Keep it basic at this level. As a rule in sales, only ask questions you know the answer to and that they know the answer to avoid getting the "no" feeling or making the prospect feel stupid, which will disable their decision-making abilities and your ability to close the sale.

3. **Opinions Transitioning Questions**
   - What are your preferences concerning . . . ?
   - What are your beliefs about . . . ?
   - What do you think about . . . ?
   - Why do you prefer that product over another?
   - How did you make your decision in the past?
   - What have you purchased before?
   - Why did you decide to contact us today?
   - Who do you usually make decisions with? Your wife?
   - How can I serve you best?

Level 4 Hopes and Dreams

Transitioning up to hopes and dreams properly is where the amateurs and the professionals are quickly separated. Creating agreement on the opinions level usually ruins most amateurs and they do not know how to transition into level 4—hopes and dreams. Hopes and dreams is future looking and if people are not comfortable at levels 1, 2, and 3, they will not answer level four truthfully.

Level four is where you find out about what the prospect wants ideally in your product or service; if they could have it their way, what would that be? Some salespeople will say, "If I could wave a magic wand, ..." which is kind of hokey but can work. At this point the client has connected with you enough to reveal what they want, or what they think they want (some men walk into car dealerships wanting a Porsche deep down but think they want a minivan as their wife instructed them to purchase).

Hopes and dreams is where you can get the client's goals, six, twelve, or eighteen months into the future, what the perfect solution would look like, what their "wish list" of benefits and features is.

4. Hopes and Dreams Transition Questions

Business

- o Where do you want to be in the next six, twelve, or eighteen months?
- o If you could design the perfect package, what would it have in it?
- o If you managed to hit that goal how would it change your life? Your business?
- o What kind of result are you looking to emulate?
- o What goals do you have for your business?

Personal

- o If you could live any way you liked, how would you like to live?
- o If you could live anywhere in the world, where would you like to live?
- o What goals do you have for your life?
- o What area of study would you like to become an expert in?
- o If you could be famous for something, what would you like to be famous for?
- o What would you like written on your tombstone? In your obituary?
- o What one thing would make you truly happy?
- o What personal qualities do you hope to develop in the future?
- o What skills do you hope to develop in your lifetime?
- o What do you dream about being the best in the world at doing?

- What are things you dream about having?
- What are things you dream about doing?
- What are things you dream about being?
- What would you do if you knew you could not fail at it?

Level 5 Feelings

Once you create agreement on Level 4, Hopes and Dreams, it's time to transition into Level 5—feelings. This is where the sale starts to get emotional and you can hook the dream, the hope, the wish, and the goal with the feelings it's going to produce from having the dream fulfilled.

You can stay on Level 5 to create a euphoric state of good feelings by future pacing what life will be like once the buyer has the result he wants. Paint a picture for the prospect, show them how awesome it's going to look in their mind, or how amazing others will think of them. Create a vivid picture that makes the client say "I want it." This is a very powerful tool for bringing the emotions up right before the crash in level 6 into fears and weaknesses.

5. **Feelings Transition Questions**
   - If we were able to deliver that result on time and on budget, how would that feel?
   - How would it feel to tell your family that you got this accomplished?
   - How are you going to feel when your boss recognizes that you made the right decision for the company?
   - How's it going to feel to put your head on the pillow tonight and know that you handled this today and it's all behind you?

Level 6 Fears and Weaknesses

This is where you transition out of the euphoric feelings of achieving the result into the pain and suffering, fears, weaknesses, deficiencies and the reality that the prospect has without your product or service.

If you have flowed nicely through levels 1–6, you will start to get some connection and some truth out of the prospect because you have followed the 7 level process properly.

Level 6 questions are meant to inflict some pain on the prospect and create a need. Excellent sales people understand how to do this as a natural part of the process. You can stack level 6 questions to create more and more pain before you relieve it in level 7.

6. **Fears, Failures, Weaknesses, Sample Questions**
   - Why hasn't this happened for you yet?
   - Why haven't you achieved that goal already?
   - What's stopping you from having that result right now?
   - Why haven't the other programs worked for you so far?
   - What are you missing to have that goal right now?
   - What's your biggest fear that is stopping you?
   - What would the worst case scenario be? Walk me through it.
   - What makes you feel like a failure?
   - What makes you feel inadequate?
   - What is your biggest fear in life?

Level 7 Needs

Once you drill down on the pain in level 6 and get the buyer to see that there is clearly a gap between where he is today and where he wants to be, this is where you start asking about his needs to relieve the pain.

Ideally, you want to get the client to say that he needs your product or service, or he needs what you are offering. If you offer coaching, you want him to say "a coach."

Once you have agreement on his needs you are at the top of the 7 Levels of agreement and you are in position to make your presentation and close the deal.

7. **Needs Sample Questions**
    - What do you need to bridge the gap between where you are and where you want to be? (Ideally get him to say your product or service)
    - What do you need to be able to make a decision today?
    - Of all the factors we spoke about today, what is the most important one to you?
    - Have I asked you everything that's important to you?
    - What do you need in order to be secure in this transaction?
    - What do you need in order to be safe?
    - What do you need in order to be significant?
    - What do you need in order to be competent?
    - What do you need in order to be powerful?
    - What do you need in order to belong?
    - What do you need to be clear about?
    - What do you need in order to build something of lasting value?
    - What do you need to feel special to others?
    - What do you need in order to feel like you are understood?
    - What do you need in order to do something great?
    - What do you need in order to achieve something that will last?
    - What recognition do you need?

Post Level 7- Level 8—Mission and The Greater Good

If you are selling in a one-to-many situation, such as a stage speaking scenario, you will have to connect on level 8 as well which is the greater good.

Level 8 is the mission, the thing that is bigger than each individual, for the sum is greater than the parts. All great speakers and leaders throughout history have banded together groups based on Level 8. For the scope of this book, we are going to keep the agreement between levels 1–7 as it's mostly designed for one-on-one sales situations.

Now, let's pause for a moment and talk about emotional quotient (EQ). Each one of us know someone who just doesn't get it when they're in a conversation, talks without listening, or talks over the client. What about those people—can they learn? The answer is, yes, if they're aware of their weaknesses and willing to. If that described you, it's time to realize you may not be as emotionally intelligent or "intuitive" as some of the natural born sales people around you, and that's okay. It's never too late to learn. In the pages to follow I'm going to give you a step-by-step guide into the proprietary process I've used in selling.

Live Action Script—Opening

<<Have energy and enthusiasm right from the start, be one notch above your prospect—not two notches, just one>>

LEVEL 1, 2, 3 clichés, facts and opinions

CLOSER: Hi, is _____ There?

BUYER: This is he.

CLOSER: This is [[YOUR FIRST AND LAST NAME]], the senior strategist from the Stefan Aarnio High Performance Company, how are you today? [[SETTER NAME]] set up this meeting today for [[TIME]] and I reviewed your application . . . Do you have quiet space, pen and paper and a computer with internet access? (*If no, reschedule the meeting—this is* *a very powerful call _____ and it could potentially be life changing so I would appreciate it if we could schedule another time to do this call; it takes anywhere from thirty minutes to an hour usually, and we need those three things: a quiet space, pen and paper, and a computer with internet access. Do you make business decisions alone or with a spouse or business partner? ((If yes, please ensure [[PARTNER NAME]] is on the call as well so we don't waste your time.))When would be better for you and I'll reset this call into my calendar).*

BUYER: Yes I do

CLOSER: Fantastic, this is going to be a powerful call today, we are going to review some of the goals that you have for real estate investing as well as some your life goals, and then if we have a fit, I'm going to go ahead and show you some of our award-winning programs that can dramatically improve your financial life; *sound fair enough?*

BUYER: Yes

CLOSER: Great, you are in good hands. Do you mind if I ask you a few questions so that I can learn more about you, where you are today, and where you want to go?

BUYER: Go ahead,

CLOSER: Fantastic, _____, how did you hear about us?

BUYER: *STOCK ANSWER—FACEBOOK*

CLOSER: Great, and what do you like about our material so far? (level 3 opinions)

CLOSER: Have you ever purchased any high-level coaching or mentoring programs before? What did you like or dislike about those programs? *(IF he has done a program before, find out what worked and didn't and most importantly—how did you make the decision to move ahead with that program over others?)*

LEVEL 4—HOPES AND DREAMS

CLOSER: Where do you want to be in real estate in the next six, twelve, or eighteen months? (*Get them to name a number of deals, or a dollar amount they would like to be earning actively in real estate. Try to nail that number down. Common numbers are $30,000, $100,000, $200,000, $250,000 and $300,000. Qualify that number with what they are earning right now, try to bring it as close to reality as possible. You can't go from $20,000 to a million overnight*)

CLOSER: If you managed to hit that goal, how would it change your life? What would you do differently?

LEVEL 5 FEELINGS

CLOSER: Imagine we got started today, and you were able to achieve that goal: how would it feel to come home and show your family the money that they earned? What do you think they would say? How would that feel?

LEVEL 6 FEARS AND WEAKNESSES

CLOSER: So _____, what has stopped you from achieving that goal in the past?

CLOSER: What's your biggest headache with your life and your business right now?

CLOSER: What would be your ideal program if you could design it?

LEVEL 7 NEEDS

CLOSER: Of all the factors we spoke about, which one do you feel is most important to you?

CLOSER: Have I asked everything that's important to you?

CLOSER: What do you *need* to bridge the gap between where you are today and where you want to go? *(Get them to say a coach, once they say coaching, now it's time to show them the presentation . . . you might have to follow up with: Would you say you need a coach to hold your hand and walk you from point A to point B making sure you are doing it right?)*

Note: You should now have their financial goal written down and now be calculating how to hit it with our programs.

PART TWO

7 LEVEL SELLING—THE ART OF A SUCCESSFUL SALES PRESENTATION

PART TWO

II

Anatomy of a Sale (Straight Line)

Your sales presentation should be scripted for mass control from opening/collection to the presentation to the close. The stronger the script, the tighter control you have over your own process, and if you are on a sales team, the management has a better time controlling the sales force and quality control in general.

**A Proper Sale
The Straight Line**

1) Opening/Collection   2) The Presentation   3) The Close

27

A good sale is straight from open to close offering no room to get off track.

Jordan Belfort, the real Wolf of Wall Street, invented the Straight-Line system that follows the correct theory of pursing the shortest path to money from opening to closing.

The salesperson controls the outcome and everything is preplanned.

NOTE: Some salespeople will violently oppose the use of scripts making claims that it makes them sound "wooden or lifeless." Scripts are 100 percent necessary for selling. You must write out your script in advance, polish it to perfection, and then keep it with you if selling over the phone. If selling in person, you must have it memorized to be effective. Natural salespeople and natural closers typically follow a framework in their head anyways. If you are a natural, you will take your sales game to the next level by scripting out your entire presentation and polishing the words until they pop from the page.

First: Write your script: opening/collection, then the presentation, then the close.

Second: Practice reading your script until you sound natural and like you aren't reading from a script

Third: Memorize and internalize your script so it becomes an unconscious competency and you don't even have to think about the mechanics.

You want to be on script to conserve your improvisational energy. A salesperson, or any person for that matter, only has a limited amount of improvisational energy a day, also known as creative or emotional energy. If you are going without a script day in and day out, you will burn out, cut corners in your presentation and eventually fail to sell anything at all. *Always use a script.*

Selling versus Negotiating

Selling and negotiating are closing related.

In my book *The Ten Commandments of Negotiation*, a negotiation has three phases like a sale and will look similar. But the main difference is that a negotiation is two-sided, and each side pushes and pulls, whereas a good sale is one-sided and goes in one direction. If you are unscripted, you run the risk of turning your sales presentation into a negotiation where the other side starts fighting back and typically, if at all, you want to reserve any negotiation for the closing sequence of the sale.

The 3C system for negotiation Collect, Clutter, Close, creates a crescendo of possibilities that balloon out in the middle of the negotiation, and that is precisely what you don't want to do in a sale. In a sale you want extreme control, so the best thing to do is have a well-scripted, rehearsed, and polished presentation to keep you on the straight line structure.

What a Negotiation Is Structured Like

Note the bulge of possibilities in the middle.

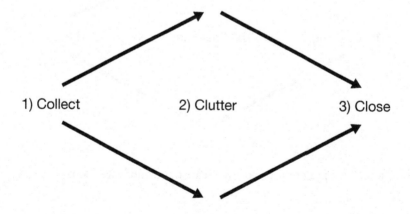

A Well-Structured Sale vs. A Badly Structured Sale

GOOD STRUCTURE—Extremely limited possibilities, closed, control, can be a lower skilled salesperson with great tools and training. Strong structure.

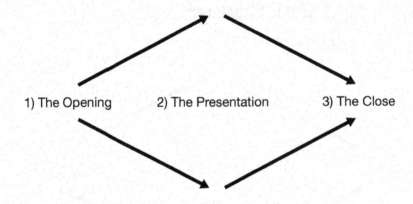

A Proper Sale
The Straight Line

1) Opening/Collection   2) The Presentation   3) The Close

BAD STRUCTURE—Too many possibilities, too open, no control, must be a natural or excellent negotiator to close with no structure.

1) The Opening   2) The Presentation   3) The Close

The 7 levels in a presentation: open, create pain, and leave them better than you found them.

To follow the 7-Level Style you used in the opening and collection, once you are on Level 7 (needs) with the prospect, it's time to build value in your sales presentation. Your presentation needs to follow the logical and emotional curve starting with clichés, building into facts, opinions, hopes and dreams, feelings and finally plunge into a pit of despair called "fears and weaknesses."

Every great salesperson is a master of creating pain and a need for what they are selling, and you are no different. Of course whoever you're selling to is in pain, because there's a gap between where they are and where they want to go and your offer (product or service) is the bridge over the gap, the medicine to their sickness that will get them to a better life.

Always leave them on a high note at the end with the feeling that future will be better than today if they would only take your offer and leave fear of loss and scarcity for not taking the offer today.

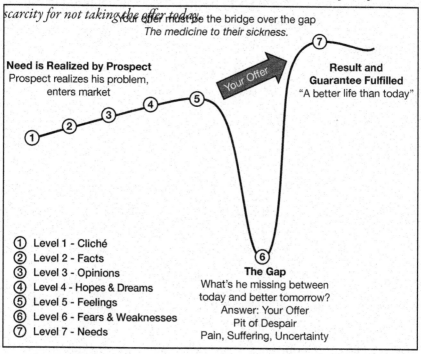

The 7 Level Presentation Curve

Your offer must be the bridge over the gap
The medicine to their sickness.

⑦

Need is Realized by Prospect
Prospect realizes his problem,
enters market

Your Offer

Result and Guarantee Fulfilled
"A better life than today"

⑤
④
③
②
①

① Level 1 - Cliché
② Level 2 - Facts
③ Level 3 - Opinions
④ Level 4 - Hopes & Dreams
⑤ Level 5 - Feelings
⑥ Level 6 - Fears & Weaknesses
⑦ Level 7 - Needs

⑥
The Gap
What's he missing between
today and better tomorrow?
Answer: Your Offer
Pit of Despair
Pain, Suffering, Uncertainty

Empowering Words and Disempowering Words

As a salesperson you are a wordsmith, and like a poet, you want to be constantly polishing, pruning, and trimming your vocabulary of weeds so you can let the true flowers grow. This is the way it is with every craft on your life's journey. You can become better if you want to.

In other words, make it your mission to remove the following words from your vocabulary:

Disempowering Words—These words are generally weak and will weaken your agreement with your prospect. They will not position you for power or influence, so eliminate them and replace them with empowering words below:

No	Pretty much
But	Sign
However	Contract
Basically	Buy

Empowering Words—These words will empower your position and will make you appear more certain and powerful while handling the prospect.

Yes and	Without a doubt
Yes and	Endorse
Yes and	Agreement
Certainty	Move ahead

When describing your product, service or offer, get used to using power words and glamour words that will make your offer seem more powerful and glamorous rather than run-of-the-mill boring words. Be intentional about your selling process, your scripts, your words and your body language. Intentionality is a process of thinking and planning in everything you do.

Insert List of Power Words

Powerful

Unparalleled

Dynamic

Innovative

Explosive

Fastest Growing

Best in class

Dramatically

Award winning

Unheard of

National Award Winner

Exclusive

Hand selected

Proven

Insert List of Glamor Words

Tremendous

Marvelous

Dazzling

Unique

Fantastic

Outstanding

New

State-of-the-art

Exciting

Artisan

Inspired

Unforgettable

Champion

Unbelievable

Real Rapport vs. Fake Rapport— Trusted Advisor, Medical Doctor

Old traditional sales books dating back almost a hundred years like *How To Win Friends and Influence People* will advise a salesperson to build rapport by finding commonality. They want you to talk about fishing, or whatever hobbies the prospect has, but at the end of the day this is fake rapport because you don't care about the prospects hobbies and they don't care that you are asking. What is common among all people looking to buy things is that they want to work with an expert.

An expert is someone who is 1) sharp as a tack 2) enthusiastic as hell 3) an expert in their field.

Think of going to see the medical doctor, who is typically a specialist who has spent ten-plus years in school and hundreds of thousands of dollars on his or her education. He or she has the shiny degrees and plaques on the wall, went to the best school—*medical school*—and is the undisputed master of his office.

The doctor makes you show up at 9:30 AM for your appointment at 10:00 AM, and at 10:15 they let you into one of the examining rooms and you wait another thirty minutes to see the doctor.

You were scheduled for 10 AM, but of course the doctor is king so the doctor shows up at 10:45 AM, forty-five5 minutes late!

The doctor asks you a short list of questions, pokes and prods you, makes a diagnosis, writes you a prescription, gives it to you, and leaves. The doctor has made a sale, and typically most people will listen to whatever the doctor said because he/she is an expert—typically sharp as a tack, enthusiastic as hell, and an expert in their field, and you don't dare question the diagnosis or the drugs they are pushing on you.

You are in rapport with the doctor because you came to see an expert and they acted like one.

Could the doctor be wrong? Absolutely, doctors are frequently wrong, but we still obey and treat them like experts and listen intently. Be the doctor. Build the rapport and be the expert. What if you entered every sales negotiation or scenario with that level of authority? In this scenario, you expect to win.

In your selling practice you want to be as specialized and as professional as a medical doctor (but never show up late for meetings) only better.

Top level salespeople in every field, whether it's real estate, financial services, insurance, car sales, etc. who run their practice to the level of professionalism of a medical doctor, study sales like a medical doctor, and invest in themselves like a medical doctor but earn money in excess of a medical doctor.

You want to be the expert and trusted advisor in your field so that your recommendations are taken like medicine just as a doctor would make a prescription.

Conscious vs. Subconscious Communication

To get into rapport with the prospect, you must be 1) sharp as a tack 2) enthusiastic as hell 3) an expert in your field.

Now you can't just come out and tell them that you are all of the above, because they would never believe you. Instead you must communicate the essence of being an expert through three things: your body language, your tone, and the words you choose to say. Walk and talk with authority. Share wisdom with authority.

A well-thought-out script can handle the words you must say, but following a script won't make you sell without proper delivery.

58 percent of communication is body language

33 percent is tone

8 percent is words used

These numbers are approximated from several sources and you may see variances on those numbers, but what remains undeniably is that words and conscious communication account for a small fraction of human communication.

What is much more important is the physiology of how we present ourselves and our body through body language and the effect on our tone of voice.

If you are selling over the phone, you eliminate body language as the prospect cannot see you (but he can hear your posture) so communication becomes nearly 80 percent tone and 20 percent words! The human brain is made up of three parts: the thinking brain or the neocortex, followed by the mammalian brain or the emotional brain, and in the middle ruling the entire brain stem is the reptilian brain which only knows fear and greed. How does this impact your sale?

Your body language and tone speak emotionally to the midbrain and lower brain and thus control the actions of the body.

The thinking brain, the neocortex cannot by itself make decisions. It can analyze, it can think, it can imagine, it can create, but it does not have decision-making power. The lower brain, namely the mammalian and reptilian brains control our decision making and our limbic system, which causes us to take action (or lack of action) on certain offers.

To master subverbal communication, you must master your tone and delivery of your pitch. A great sales presentation is both logical and emotional, and no matter how beautifully you craft the words, if you do not perform them like a professional actor would deliver a script on stage, the words won't matter without delivery. Delivery is everything. Do you pause at just the right moment? Do you ask questions? Do you give the human in the other end a moment to share, and make small talk—which is a nervous function but also an autopilot function of nearly every human when they talk?

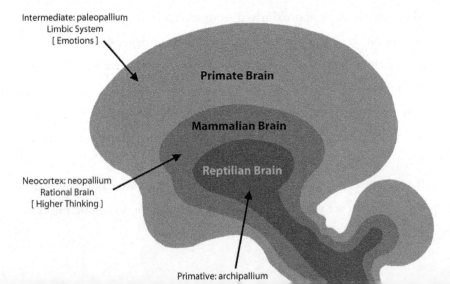

Intermediate: paleopallium
   Limbic System
   [Emotions]

Primate Brain

Mammalian Brain

Reptilian Brain

Neocortex: neopallium
   Rational Brain
   [Higher Thinking]

Primative: archipallium

Tone Training

All top salespeople have one thing in common—they all sound amazing! Whether you are a natural salesperson or worked hard to become proficient, all salespeople share the same commonality of having tremendously shaped tone and almost a musical sound to how they communicate over the phone and in person. It's almost as if they could sell an Eskimo an igloo in the Bahamas. You want to listen to their voice and tone forever.

This makes logical sense when you consider that the tone of voice is subverbal communication which accounts for nearly all of the brain's emotional decision-making power, and people buy on emotions, not logic!

Consider the opposite—poor salespeople with low charisma and a low likability factor usually misuse tone. They may be too flat, too wooden, too forced, too fake, wrong amounts of energy at the wrong times, and overall the words, tone and body language do not create a congruent picture. Congruent means it must line up in the prospect's mind. If things don't "line up" or "make sense" or "something is off," the bad gut feeling will start to creep in, and the emotional brain will want to fight or take flight. In sales, your prospects will flee if you have bad tone, or they will "call you back later," which they never will.

Tone allows you to communicate the emotion that you care about the prospect, you care about his situation, you are a human being too, you understand his pains and struggles and rather than being tossed aside like some kind of-cheap overseas telemarketer with a canned, robotic "Hello sir, may I speak to Mr. Smith?" You will rather be welcomed as an "old friend" on a subconscious level.

Tone is so fundamental to mammal communication that babies, dogs, children, people who do not speak your language, and other life forms that don't have a grasp of "words" of the English language can still communicate effectively with tone and gestures alone. Tone is the key to speaking to the emotional brain, and if you want to be a master salesperson, you must master your use of tone.

Overall there are twenty-nine types of tonality used in human communication, but ten core influencing types of tone. In your sales career you must study and master these types of tone to give your scripts and presentations the warm, musical, "I care" feeling, that the majority of salespeople fail to ever achieve.

10 Core Influencing Types of Tone As identified by Jordan Belfort

1. **"I care," "I really want to know"**—upbeat enthusiasm, genuine curiosity
2. **Declarative as question**—Raise the inflection at the end of a statement to imply a question. This forces the listeners mind to "listen in" because tonally they have been asked a question, but in words, they have been told a statement. Used frequently in opening scripts: "Hey, is this John? . . . Hi my name is Bill Smith, calling from the ABC Company, in Winnipeg, Manitoba."
3. **Mystery/intrigue**—Lower your voice as if to tell a secret that are only letting them in on.
4. **Scarcity**—Lower your voice *just* above a whisper, with a sense of urgency and scarcity.
5. **Absolute certainty**—A firmer, more definitive tone of power and certainty from the solar plexus, conviction.
6. **Utter sincerity**—Velvety smooth, almost apologetic, calm, confident, low pressure, sincere at the highest possible level.
7. **Reasonable man**—I'm reasonable, your reasonable, this is a reasonable request.

8. **Hypothetical money-aside**—hypothetically speaking, money aside, does the idea make sense to you?

9. **Implied obviousness**—It's beyond obviousness that your product or service is a winner.

10. **"I feel your pain"**—Complete and utter sincerity, used to identify primary and secondary pain points. The "Bill Clinton" tone.

Learn, master, and memorize these types of tone and apply them to your opening, presentation, and closing scripts like a musical composer would add dynamics like "loud, soft, quickly, slowly, staccato, etc." to his music. Mastering the right tone at the right time is something that the clear majority of salespeople completely ignore, especially if they haven't scripted their presentation and are using mental energy to improvise. When it comes to selling, delivery is more important than mechanics. Master your tone, and you will master delivery.

Disabling the Conscious Mind—The Neocortex

As a salesperson, you can only speak between 100–200 words per minute, but the subconscious human mind races at 500 words per minute. This is called the internal monologue your prospect is having with himself during all parts of your sales encounter. Always be mindful of his fears, hesitations, and limiting beliefs.

You might say "Our product is best in class" and the prospect will nod in agreement, but his subconscious says, "Says who! Yeah right, this thing is probably a piece of crap and this is just another sales guy."

You cannot speak fast enough at 100 words per minute to compete with the 500 word per minute subconscious mind, so a master salesperson does not compete with the subconscious mind; instead he disables it in one of three ways.

1. **Tell a story**—Facts tell, stories sell. When you begin presenting your offer your prospect's analytical neocortex will be racing against you to refute and challenge any claims you make. You may get someone so wrapped up in facts that they are operating completely in their neocortex and "have to think about it" or "have to crunch the numbers." This is called an analyst frame, and it is death to your sale because the neocortex is unable to make a decision; those decisions are controlled by the mammalian and reptilian brains. To disable the analyst frame, you can put it to bed by telling it a story. The most powerful type of story is a third-party story about how others had success, perhaps a case study, client testimonial, how others made decisions in the past, the story about the client who missed out, the story of the client who waited too long, the story of the old widow who never got married because she waited until it was the right time. For millennia, humans have remembered and told stories to transmit major tribal and life information. The Vikings had the Sagas, the Christians have the New Testament of the Bible, the Greeks had the Odyssey, the Romans had the Aeneid, and inside these epic stories were lessons on life. Many of these epic stories are still around today because human brains are wired to remember complex information through stories. Analytics and numbers will always be forgotten at some point, but stories are forever.

2. **Ask a question**—One of the fastest ways to disable the conscious mind is to ask it a question. When you are speaking, the conscious mind of your prospect is hammering away at 500 words per minute, but when you ask it a question, the words per minute goes to zero, and all of their processing power goes into finding an answer, not judging or challenging you and your claims. Questions are powerful because they not

only disable the conscious mind but also make the prospect feel more involved in the process and engages them.

Two rules about asking questions:

Rule #1: Never ask a question they don't know the answer to: this threatens the prospect, creates the "no" feeling, challenges them, breaks rapport, breaks agreement, and can send your sale into a death spiral where the prospect feels stupid and can't find enough confidence to make a decision. A confused mind doesn't buy. If they don't know the answer to the question, feed it to them subtly in advance. For example, "My dear old friend, John Smith, has eight kids . . . How many kids does he have?" The prospect says, "Eight." You say, "That's exactly right!"

Rule #2 of asking questions: Never ask a question you don't know the answer to and the prospect doesn't know the answer to. This can completely derail and destroy your sale. Many amateur salespeople will ask a question that neither they nor the prospect know an answer to, and this can send the presentation into chaos. Don't take the risk; choose your questions well. If they don't know the answer, give it to them in advance or give them options to choose from: "Would you prefer red or blue?"

3. **Speak to their internal monologue**—Now obviously you cannot only ask questions and tell stories throughout the entire sale; there are parts to the sale like the closing process, the opening process, the presentation etc. where you do not have the luxury of telling pure stories or asking pure questions. So instead, to control the conscious mind, you want to tailor your presentation and your close to what the prospect is likely to be thinking anyways. This can take some practice; you may have to record yourself presenting and watch yourself over and over again from the other side to develop the internal monologue that the prospect will have. If you can speak to their concerns and objections as they form during a presentation

or during a close, the prospect will say, "Wow, this guy is reading my mind! He knows exactly what I want and he gets me, I trust him, I'm in." This is a major trust builder: if you can get your presentation to the point where you can read the prospects mind in advance, the same way a chess grandmaster sees eight moves ahead, you can see the future as well with a well scripted, rehearsed, and planned sales presentation.

Irrational Hot Buttons

In the movie *Saving Mr. Banks*, Tom Hanks, who plays Walt Disney, is trying to purchase the movie rights to the famous book *Mary Poppins* from P. L. Travers during the 1960s when Disney as an empire is rolling out hit after hit and Walt Disney appears to be on a conquest to own every single great children's story across the landscape, musicalize it, and turn it into a movie. His young daughter loves the book *Mary Poppins*, as it brings her so much joy, and Disney, as a good father, promises his daughter that he will bring that small children's story to the big screen. For twenty years, Disney pitches Travers persistently over and over again in different ways trying to buy the script through any means necessary.

The movie opens with Travers entering financial hardship: her bank accounts are running out, she lets her staff go, and she is in jeopardy of losing her house. Financially, her book royalties have dried up, and a movie deal with Disney is the next logical business and financial move for her. The movie deal would not only be logical, but it would be a windfall and catapult her to even greater success.

Finally, Disney flies Travers to his offices in Los Angeles and in good faith, has the entire movie script for *Mary Poppins* made in advance: character and scene sketches are done, and he has a great poet and composer on staff to make the iconic songs for the movie. All Travers must do is agree to sell the movie rights by signing one piece of paper, and she will get the biggest financial windfall of her life.

Travers shows up and she is a miserable, old, crusty English lady who is completely disagreeable to everything America and the core beliefs Disney stands for. In fact, she seems to have a hate for musicals, music, cartoons and everything Disney—even Mickey Mouse! Walt Disney spends the entire movie selling, negotiating, reselling, reselling, and reselling the vision and the idea until finally the real issue is revealed. Travers loves her characters and doesn't want to give up Mary Poppins because she loves "her" but more importantly Mr. Banks who represents her father in real life, who was a nice guy, but a horrible drunk that ruined her family.

Disney wanted to portray Mr. Banks as his own father figure, a banker with a moustache who was stern, not fun, took care of the family but was absent. Travers wanted Mr. Banks remembered as a fun loving, nice guy with no facial hair, like her father.

The crux of sale happens when Travers refuses to sign the movie rights and flies home to England to sit in her house as her money runs out and she slowly lose everything. Disney, on good faith, flies to England, shows up at the door, and realizes that Travers's hot button is that she wants Mr. Banks to be remembered as a nice and fun man, so finally a Disney changes the ending of the movie from a cold Mr. Banks ending to an alternate where Mr. Banks comes home a nice guy and flies a kite with his family, thus the hit song "Let's Go Fly a Kite."

Travers is sold, she remembered her father as being the kind of guy who would do such a thing, and reluctantly she sells the movie rights.

The moral of the story is that people do not make rational decisions. Travers, the author, was broke, almost bankrupt, and on the edge of losing her house, and still she refused to sign her movie rights over to one of the most successful film makers of all time because of her hot button—her love for her father. In fact, her real name was Helen Goff but changed her name to (P. L. Travers) with Travers being the name of her father. The entire sale was made and the negotiation was won because Disney understood the value of Travers's hot button, and when he found it, it he pushed it as hard as he could and made movie history with the hit movie *Mary Poppins*.

People never buy on rationality; they buy rather on "hot buttons" and irrational thinking. Therefore if you can understand their triggers immediately, you will understand their underlying drivers or needs.

People put their dogs in "doggy spas" to make them feel good about their dog. The dog does not care or maybe even know he's in a spa. The dog won't say "thank you" or express his gratitude, but the owner does it because the dog is a hot button.

They say the man in the church and the man in the bar are looking for the same thing—to belong to something. It's the salesperson's job to provide that belonging and meet that need.

Hot buttons can be anything, and if you can identify what they are in the questioning phase, you can satisfy the irrational need.

Some hot buttons might be color, size, brand, shape, white glove service, guarantees, warranties, pets, children, spouses, girlfriends/boyfriends, to belong, to contribute, to be remembered, get laid, get paid, live forever, youth, health, beauty, loyalty, a relationship, and too many more to list.

Hot buttons typically come from the prospect's desire for status, respect, recognition, personal prestige, or enjoyment. However one of the most common mistakes a salesperson makes is to view the prospect through the lens of their own thinking. Rookies do this all the time. Do not assume you know a person's hot button in advance, because you will only find it through proper questioning, and once you find it, push it!

The Risk of Presenting Features and Benefits That Are of No Interest to the Customer

By default, most average salespeople overtime without a script degrade their presentation down to a series of features, benefits, and price and will rely on a guarantee to close. In general no one cares about the features—ever. What we all want are the benefits.

Getting stuck on features is a trap and typically, unless the prospect asks more about a certain feature or benefit, he doesn't care. What is paramount above all things is the result and the guarantee.

This does not mean that you don't explain any of the features to your prospect, but you need to find out what is important to him, not to you. Too many salespeople are thinking about what is important to them, rather than what's important to the customer.

In the wise words of Warren Buffet, "What you love about you is your hobby; what others love about you is your business."

You don't want to go ranting about the ease of online access when the customer replies, "I'm old, I don't go online." In that case you want to talk about written materials, hard media, and something the customer can actually use. When you present features of no value, you will quickly lose rapport with and the interest of the customer.

To quickly assess what type of person you are dealing with, generally there are four types of buyers who speak four different languages:

Speaking Their Language—Four Personality Styles

Understand that there are four types of buyers out in the world, and each buyer has a specific language that he speaks. If you approach the right buyer with the right language, you will be able to communicate. In contrast, if you have the wrong language for the wrong type of person, you will have major difficulties in striking a deal.

Typically speaking, when making a sales presentation, you need to appeal to all four personality styles at once because you do not know who you are really dealing with. This applies in a magnified way with selling to groups of people. You have no idea who is in the audience and your ability to check in with every single person becomes impossible.

DISC—Dominance, Influence, Submission, and Compliance

The DISC system was created by **William Moulton Marston** in 1928 when he published the book *"Emotions of Normal People.* The History of DISC began with the elements of Fire, Earth, Air, and Water. The theory behind these four quadrants of personality style was originally written by Empodocles in 444 B.C.

Intuitively we know that there are four different types of people. If you watch any TV sitcom or any movie there are always these same four types of characters played over and over again. Whether it's the Simpsons (Homer, Marge, Lisa, Bart) or Seinfeld (Jerry, Elaine, George, Kramer), there are always four types of people that are balanced out by one another.

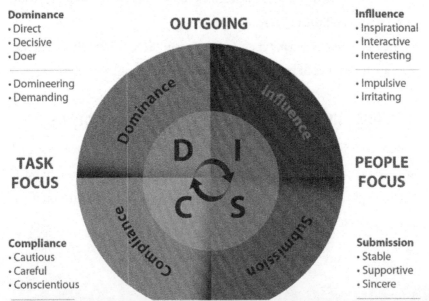

Dominance
- Direct
- Decisive
- Doer

- Domineering
- Demanding

OUTGOING

Influence
- Inspirational
- Interactive
- Interesting

- Impulsive
- Irritating

TASK FOCUS

PEOPLE FOCUS

Compliance
- Cautious
- Careful
- Conscientious

Submission
- Stable
- Supportive
- Sincere

Dominance—5 percent of the population. These are your fire, police, military, and business leaders. They are outgoing and task oriented, and D is for direct. These people are results focused and want to get down to the bottom line immediately. They are task focused and seek to control their surroundings. They also believe that they are more powerful than their surroundings and believe that their surroundings are hostile. Dominance types are not interested in making friends, nor are they are not interested in holding hands and singing "Kumbayah." They ask straight questions and want straight results. When you communicate with a D-type, deliver straight communication, give it to them straight, and give them results. If they were to choose a vehicle they would likely choose a Mercedes, and their favorite color would be black—the color of dominance.

Influence—35 percent of the population. High I-types are your natural sales people, advertising, marketing, public relations, tourism, retail, comedians and onstage performers. These people are outgoing and people oriented, I stands for Influence. I-types want to see and be seen and they want to be friends, want to be liked, drink wine, have lunch, drive the convertible around, live a great lifestyle, have fun, and speak in public. I-types believe they are more powerful than their surroundings and believe that their surroundings are friendly. When communicating with an I-type, deliver them the sizzle, not the steak. They want to know how fast, fun, exciting and cool looking the new idea is. They also want everyone to know how great it will look for them to make this new decision. If they were to choose a vehicle, they would choose the sexy convertible and their favorite color would be red—a hot, flashy, look-at-me color.

Submission—35 percent of the population—S-types are your teachers, nurses, administrative, supporters, finance, HR, manufacturing, and generally nice people. They want stable, steady, supportive, and sincere communication. S-types also love guarantees, want to feel safe, secure, and legitimacy in a transaction. They perceive the environment to be more powerful than they are and perceive the environment to be friendly. They are reserved people-people and are not necessarily outgoing like the high I-types. When doing business with S-types they want the right thing and they want to make sure that no one is getting hurt. If they were to choose a vehicle it would likely be a minivan that could fit all of their friends and pets. Their favorite color of choice would be blue because it is calm and steady.

Satisfying professions for the 4 personalities

D-Style 5% of the population

- Entrepreneurs
- Sales – Full Commission
- Sales Management
- Legal / Litigation
- Operations Management

I-Style 35% of the population

- Advertising / Marketing
- Public Relations
- Training
- Sales
- Hospitality / Tourism
- Retail – Sales

C-Style 25% of the population

- Accounting / Auditing
- Engineering
- Research and Development
- Quality Assurance / Safety
- Architecture
- Computer Programming

S-Style 35% of the population

- Teaching / Education
- Finance / Economics
- Human Resources
- Administration / Support Svcs
- Retail – Customer Service
- Manufacturing

Compliance—25 percent of the population—C-types are engineers, accountants, attorneys, doctors, accountants, architects and computer programmers. These people want statistics, facts, and figures. They do not want to know that roughly half of the time the program is successful; they want to know that 48.34 percent of the time the program is successful. These people perceive the environment to be more powerful than them and that the environment is hostile. They are reserved, task oriented individuals who want to make decisions based on facts, figures, and statistics. When they make a decision, they want to back it up with cold hard data and logic. If a compliance person were to choose a vehicle it would be a van or a truck because of the utility and usefulness and ability to haul things (even if they rarely haul goods), and their favorite color is irrelevant because it isn't statistically measurable.

When you meet the prospect, you must very quickly determine what type of person you are dealing with so that you can speak their language. Very quickly you can determine if they are outgoing or reserved and if they are people oriented or task oriented. From those to quick questions you can determine where they fit on the DISC axis.

People vs. Task based and Outgoing vs. Reserved?

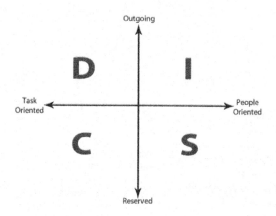

Analyzing the GAP between Where They Are and Where They Want to Be

When you are moving your prospect up through the levels of agreement from 1–7:

7 Levels of Agreement

1. Clichés
2. Facts
3. Opinions
4. Hopes and Dreams

5. Feelings
6. Fears and Weaknesses
7. Needs

When you get into Level 6 and drill down on fears, weaknesses, things that are missing, pain points, and problems, that is where the gap between hopes and dreams, what they really want, and where they are today emerges.

The 7 Level Presentation Curve

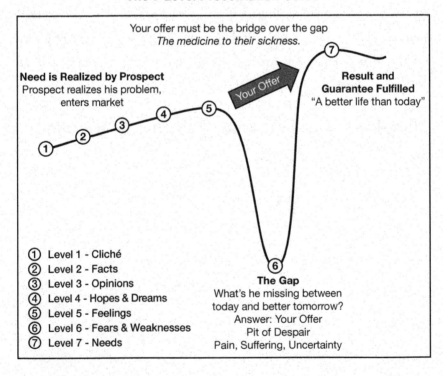

Your offer must be the bridge over the gap
The medicine to their sickness.

⑦

Need is Realized by Prospect
Prospect realizes his problem,
enters market

Your Offer

Result and Guarantee Fulfilled
"A better life than today"

④ ⑤

③

②

①

⑥

The Gap
What's he missing between
today and better tomorrow?
Answer: Your Offer
Pit of Despair
Pain, Suffering, Uncertainty

① Level 1 - Cliché
② Level 2 - Facts
③ Level 3 - Opinions
④ Level 4 - Hopes & Dreams
⑤ Level 5 - Feelings
⑥ Level 6 - Fears & Weaknesses
⑦ Level 7 - Needs

Ultimately, the prospect realizes the gap between where he is now and where he wants to be and you can see the gap as well.

So you might feed him a level 6 question like "Why hasn't this result happened for you yet?"

The prospect may be forthcoming enough to answer honestly, but typically, they will blame an outside force: "It wasn't a priority," "I never focused on it," "Haven't had the time/money/education etc."

The prospect in most cases does *not* say, "Because I need your service now; here's my credit card."

So you might probe him with a few more level 6 questions to really get to the root of the pain and then you will ask a level 7 question, "What do you need to close the gap between where you are and where you want to be?"

The ideal answer to the question for you would be "A system," "A path to follow," "A coach," "Your product," "Your service," or something along those lines. If they say your product or something in your industry, even better.

The trouble with closing the gap is that it means different things to all different people; to get the gap into common terms you need to convert it into time and money. A certain amount of money and time goes in, and a certain amount of time and money is saved or generated in return. Everybody understands time and money, which are essentially interchangeable and in some ways the same thing—stored human energy.

People do not buy products or services; they buy results and guarantees. A product will get you a result. For example, you may go to the hardware store to buy a drill because you need a hole to put a screw in to hang a new piece of art you bought. You don't want the drill, you want the result—the picture hung! And while you are searching for this result you are looking for the greatest guarantee against risk of loss.

Rule: Never Be the Lowest Cost Provider
Instead Be the Lowest Risk Provider.

You never want to fight for the bargain basement; discounting is a flawed strategy and usually a race to the bottom of low profits. The key to selling and closing the gap is to not be the lowest cost provider of that result and guarantee, but rather the lowest risk provider.

Warren Buffet, world's richest investor, has a portfolio of not just companies he invests in, but typically he invests in the preferred brands and tastes of the customer. For example he owns Coca Cola, McDonalds, Dairy Queen, Snickers, and branded items that are intimate with the customer. Customers are intimate with those items because they put them in their mouths, smell them, taste them and know they deliver a strong promise of delivery. The customer does not want the risk of drinking a No Name Cola or eating at Jim's Burger Dive, or going to Dairy Ice Cream Shop or eating a no-name candy bar. People buy the brands because of the low risk provided and typically pay a price premium for that brand guarantee.

Maybe you have a brand and a relationship with trust and a guarantee to the prospect, or maybe you don't have an established brand, but either way, you want to have a strong promise, guarantee, or warranty behind your result.

So the equation in the prospect's mind is:

Cost (Money + Time + Energy) in + Value (Result + Guarantee) = Life will be better tomorrow (More Future Money + Time + Energy for the Customer)

Your job when closing the gap is to get in the cost of the problem at hand, the pain into monetary terms. You can try a level 6 question like "What's it costing you right now to not implement this system?"

You also want to get the future value into monetary terms and build the value so that it is ten times the cost if possible. That creates an airtight logical case for the value of your offer. You can get your value to ten times by talking about lifetime value of your result—not only in terms of savings from the pain, but time, money, and energy saved, found, and created by having the proper result today.

By default, if you haven't built the value, analyzed the gap, and established the result and the guarantee in monetary terms, your offer, no matter how good, will always be viewed as 10/10 costly and 3/10 valuable on its own.

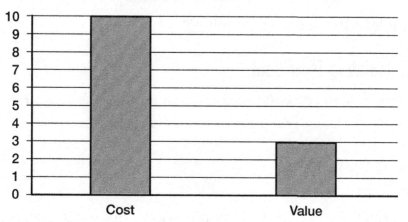

Low Value High Cost

Your job as a salesperson is to reverse the cost and value so that the value is built in analyzing the gap and getting it into real money terms so that the prospect can compare the lifetime costs of not having the result today and future earnings/savings from having the result.

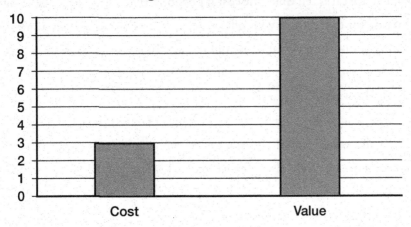

Work on your presentation, your value stack, and putting your prospect's gap into real money terms. This will help you close the gap.

Calculating Their Goal

Average Median Home Price (get them to say the number, help them if they are off) * 10 percent = Net profit using our system

You can google the median home price while on the phone with them or know it beforehand

CLOSER: So _____ From what have told me so far, your goal is to make $200,000 in the next twelve to eighteen months to get out of your job. Now what do you think the average home price is in your local market of [[THEIR CITY]]?

BUYER: $300,000

CLOSER: Exactly! The median home in your city is $300,000 and that's just a run of the mill average single family home. Now using our exact system of buying real estate at 40–60 cents on the dollar, fixing it to 70 cents on the dollar, selling at 100 cents on the dollar, costing you ten cents to sell, and making you 20 cents on the dollar, after everything is said and done, you should be able to put at least ten cents in your pocket, so what's 10 percent of $300,000 . . . ?

BUYER: $30,000 of course.

CLOSER: Exactly right, so from my quick analysis, we are going to need between six to twelve deals a year to hit your income goal of 200k. Make sense?

We now have all of the necessary information to move into the presentation phase and later into a strong closing position because we ended up on level 7.

From this information we can find the right program for the prospect.

Presenting Your Offer—Value vs. Cost: Value First, Cost Second

> *"Price is what you pay, value is what you get."*
> —Warren Buffet

When it comes time to present your offer in real money terms, you are asking the prospect to give up something of value to him for something of value to him in return. Price is what you pay, value is what you get, and if the value is not built or understood, prospects only hear cost.

Cost is time, effort, energy, and money in, and thus you always want to present your offer so the value is first and the cost is second.

When the customer inquires, "How much is it?" the wrong answer is "$3,000." This answer is weak because the customer only sees price; he doesn't see the value.

A better answer is "For a cash outlay of only $3,000 john, my company will be delivering over $10,000 of results over a period of X time in Y method with Z guarantee/warranty."

When the value is higher than the cost, people buy. When the value is lower than the cost (or risk) they don't buy.

A Punishing Amount of Evidence: Testimonials and Whitepapers

Bill Bartmann was the founder of a company called CFS based out of Oklahoma, USA. CFS, which stood for "Commercial Financial Services," was at the time the biggest collection agency in the USA with 3,900 employees and revenues in the billions. Prior to Bill's career in collections, he was a family lawyer and knew the power of written evidence. Bill's USP—unique selling proposition to the market place with his company—was to be "the good guys" of the charged off debt collection business. At the time, most collection companies in the industry, except for Bill's, would use abuse, scare tactics, yelling, swearing, name calling, threats, and anything nasty to collect a debt. Bill had been bankrupt himself and had seen the dark side of this industry when a debt collector called his house and his little daughter picked up the phone to hear that her "daddy was a deadbeat."

Something had to change. Bill reversed the collection process and went from being the meanest to the friendliest. Rather than working against people, he worked with good people to get them back on their feet. The way Bill operated was 180 degrees different from the corrupt and dirty industry and because he served the public in a different way, for which he would o collect love letters and testimonials.

Bill, as a lawyer, compiled all of the testimonials into a binder called the "5-pounder" (he in fact had several of them) and of course being in the collection business, people would try to sue Bill and his company often. He would get attacks, and when he would show up to court, he would "bring out the 5-pounder" and lay it down on the desk in front of the judge with a line-up of satisfied customers who would testify in his defense. Bill knew the power of overwhelming evidence and that you need more than one case to deliver your point; you needed 1,000 cases to create absolute certainty to the public that he was the good guy.

You don't need one case to prove your point; you need 1,000 cases and an overwhelming amount of evidence. Do whatever you need to do to collect testimonials from every customer; all it takes is one attack against you, your company, or your name, and you will need to pull out your own "5 pounder" of overwhelming evidence that you are everything you claim to be.

When showing prospects testimonials in a presentation, I would rather show too many than too few. Presenting more evidence—and especially overwhelming evidence—is one way to silence the doubts in a prospect's mind that you are able to deliver on your result and guarantee.

Sales literature to back up your claims is one of the most powerful sales tools you can have when presenting. Everything you say is heresy, and everything the prospect says is reality in the eyes of the customer. To add an aura of legitimacy to your presentation it is almost essential, even in the modern digital world, to have printed materials. For whatever reason, the power of the written word—and namely, the printed word—is more powerful than the digital word or any other word, for that matter.

Here are the three most powerful types of sales literature you can have in your arsenal:

1. **A published book**—The most effort required and resources to generate—This book could be about you or your company; several companies are now getting books into their sales and marketing to help them sell their services

2. **Whitepapers**—The second most effort required and resources to generate—Case studies of successful clients filled with how the product and service worked for them. Prospects love to see "someone just like them" succeeding with your product or service. Their mind needs to find evidence that not only "this works," but "this can work for me," and people seem to always think they are different. In your white papers, case studies, and testimonials show all different types of people succeeding, different ages, genders, backgrounds, races, advanced customers, starter customers, etc. so there is something for everyone.

3. **Glossy sales materials created by the marketing department**— Virtually no effort to generate—Anything your company creates will immediately be taken as untrustworthy. It all looks nice and commands legitimacy, but people no longer trust marketing also known as: what you say about you. They are more interested in what others have to say about you in today's current market economy. Still with all the downsides, the customer will find you to be more legitimate if you have the glossy brochure to visually "show them what they get." Spending money on print is still (and likely always) will be worth it.

The Power of a Video Testimonial

In today's market the leading edge of technology is digital video, and nothing is more emotional than watching an actual customer express the gratitude, the pain they felt before the result, and hearing their story first-hand. Videos can tell stories visually, and they put people into "story mode" and out of analytical mode especially if they are well done and professionally produced.

There are two types of video testimonials that are valuable to you:

1. Quick, dirty, easy, guerrilla style videos of prospects telling you about their experience in an authentic "real" way. We live in an age where there is too much polish on too many presentations, and sometimes a quick and dirty video testimonial can be refreshing. However, the picture and sound usually isn't great, so if it's all you have, you look unprofessional

2. High production professional videos—These will cost you money; offer to pay to have them done. Camera crews today are cheaper than ever before, and equipment is cheaper than ever before. The guy who shoots my video also shoots professional footage for Chrysler-Dodge commercials, and he can be hired for a couple hundred dollars. The advantage to using polished video is that the audio quality is perfect, you can add music to pump the emotions, and you can cut and control the shots and show not just the customer but also create an emotional montage. You can display stats such as "cash invested" and "cash earned," and you can write down key benefits on the screen. Having at least a few high-production testimonials will immediately set you out from the pack as few salespeople are willing to spend the money to have an outstanding testimonial.

TIP: You can create a sales tool website of just testimonials, video, written, screen shots, amateur video—everything you collect becomes your own "5 pounder" and overwhelming evidence that you can deliver on your promises.

When I first got into business and selling I used to think that testimonials were cheesy, manufactured, and that no one really cared or believed them. I was wrong! There is an entire subset of customers that are exclusively looking for testimonials, and if they can't find any, they won't buy. On the flip side, there are customers who do not care about testimonials. When presenting, you never know who you are dealing with, so you are better to be on the side of overwhelming evidence rather than underwhelming evidence.

Creating Agreement and Momentum Towards The Close

All effective sales presentations need stopping off points where you can "check in" with the customer to make sure he's following so you can gain commitment. In a one-on-one setting, this is easy because you can see him nodding or read his body language and gauge interest from there. In a group or over the phone, you are going to have to ask for agreement with a series of close-ended questions that are going to bring you into a series of "yesses" that build momentum towards the close. The more yesses the customer gives you before the close, the harder it is for him to say no and kill the rapport of the sale. This is where you want to have two major special devices to create agreement and hit the close with as much momentum as possible.

Tie Downs—Create agreement by using statements followed by shouldn't it, wouldn't it, couldn't it, isn't he, isn't she, aren't they?

Example 1:

Salesperson: Most of our clients see results in eight weeks or less; that would be great, wouldn't it?

Prospect: Yeah, of course!

Example 2:

Salesperson: John was able to see fantastic results from our program and was able to take his two little girls to Disneyland this past winter for Christmas, and he sent me this picture of his family. They sure do you look happy, don't they?

Prospect: Yeah, they do look great.

Example 3:

The Nested Tie down—Put your tie down at the middle of the statement instead of the end.

Salesperson: The average profit you should see would be $30,000 per transaction; wouldn't it be great to take that to the bank today?

Prospect: Ha ha, I'd love it!

Example 4:

Reverse Tie Down–

Salesperson: <opens the car door to a brand new BMW and the client sits down in the brand new leather interior> Doesn't it feel amazing?

Prospect: Yeah, it's amazing . . .

Trial Closes—The second type of tool to use are trial closes, which are typically close-ended questions to gain commitment and see if the prospect is on board before going for the final close, which is very simply asking for the business.

Some examples of common trial closes:

a. How does this sound to you?
b. Does this make sense to you so far?
c. Would this feature be useful to your current operations?
d. Do you like this color?
e. Would this be an improvement on what you are doing right now?
f. Is this what you had in mind?
g. Do you like the value?
h. Do you like the idea?

The 7 Level Presentation Process

The 7-Level Presentation Process needs to show the product or service also known as the offer as the perfect fit for the client's needs both logically and emotionally. It must fit in with all seven levels of agreement, clichés, facts, opinions, hopes and dreams, feelings, fears and weaknesses, and lastly needs.

The presentation must be scripted to avoid salespeople from destroying the sale by saying "stupid things." Scripts are one of the most powerful sales tools because they allow anyone in any region in the company to give a standard presentation and avoid saying stupid things. How else would a rookie salesperson know? Even the most seasoned salesperson needs solid training and coaching. A script helps alleviate unknowns.

When salespeople run out of intelligent things to say, they start saying stupid things, which are either 1) true and sound stupid or 2) untrue and are lies. When there is no script in place, you run the risk of sales people saying stupid things, which can get you into major trouble with regulatory bodies if you are in a regulated industry like investments, real estate, mortgages, insurance, etc.

Live Action Script—Platinum Presentation

CLOSER: Now _____, you told me that your goal this year was to become a fulltime real estate investor and you also told me that the amount of money you needed to make was $200,000 to make that happen, right?

BUYER: Yes.

CLOSER: Okay, well if you could open up a webpage for me, StefanAarnio. com/coaching I'll show you some of the coaching options that would work for you. Let me know when it's loaded . . .

BUYER: It's loaded.

CLOSER: Do you see where it says "implementation coaching"?

BUYER: Yup, I see it.

CLOSER: Scroll down a little more to where you see the Harvard Principle. See it? Great, before we get started I want to tell you a little bit about the Harvard Principle. You see _____ Harvard is the best university in the world because they attract the best students. Our program is very similar, and in fact, we make sure that we only attract the very best to our programs. You can see there is a three-step process to qualify for coaching and we are on step 2 right now. I'm trying to find out on this call if you are the right guy for this program and if you can actually succeed with what we give you.

Do you think you're the right guy? (either answer yes or no) Okay, we'll see. Now our program has a success rate that is nearly ten times the industry average. Most companies in our industry have a 3–5 percent success rate, but ours is hovering around 47 percent because we deliver a superior training program and attract superior people; make sense?

BUYER: Yup.

CLOSER: Now there are two programs I had in mind for you that would help you bridge that gap from where you are now to where you want to be at the $200,000 of earnings. (*Always show the higher ticket program first and down sell to the lower. This prospect qualifies for Gold or Platinum packages.*)

CLOSER: The one I want to start with is the absolute best we have to offer, the Platinum program. Do you see it on the screen there? Fantastic. Now the Platinum program is our award-winning professional program because in 2016 Dan Nagy was the winner of Investor of the Year by *Canadian Real Estate Wealth* magazine. Since then, we have had several other graduate Platinum students nominated for awards!

CLOSER: I want you to write this down, _____. The program is designed to be delivered in a twelve-month time frame, but some students stretch it out to eighteen months; it's up to you and it's session-based, so there is no time limit once you are in the program, but we recommend you get everything done in the shortest timeframe possible. It's kind of like when the doctor prescribes you a bottle of medicine to take in a week—if you take the pills in a week, you get the result, but if you drag it out too long, the medicine doesn't work.

CLOSER: How we deliver the value to you is through forty-eight weekly accountability sessions over the phone with one of our coaches who is a full time professional real estate investor. These people are full-time business people and part-time coaches, so you don't have to worry about some bum coach in a call center coaching you for $10 an hour who doesn't know anything. These coaches are hand selected by Stefan himself, and they have been trained in our program.

CLOSER: The beauty with the calls every week is that we never let you get off track; you might have a bad week or two, but the momentum keeps you going; makes sense?

BUYER: Yes.

CLOSER: Fantastic, now with that, we give you four full days on site with your coach, and typically you want to take one of those every quarter so that you can take your business to the next level. The one-day sessions are really powerful because you get to go onsite with your coach into the field and see how it's done, and most people don't believe it until they see it. Usually after a student has a one-day, there is a huge breakthrough, and many get their first deal or go to the next level. Makes sense?

BUYER: Yes.

CLOSER: Now we also give you our full set of mastery classes and box sets, and if you scroll down a little more can you see where it says "Self-Made Academy"?

BUYER: Yes.

CLOSER: That's our five-course curriculum of live classes that you get included to sharpen your skills so that you can hit your goal. You get all five. With Raising Capital, most people who take that class raise at least $1,000,000 within the year and many of the Platinum students raise between $3,000,000 to $5,000,000. Negotiations are for learning how to buy at 40–60 cents on the dollar, and Marketing, Sales and, of course, Advanced Buy-Fix-Sell. We focus on the soft skills and the core skills that are going to get you to six and seven figures *fast* rather than the nuts and bolts of real estate in those classes. Makes sense?

BUYER: Yes.

CLOSER: For each of those you get two tickets to the three-day class held every six months and we run it on a 2.5 year rotation so you will be taking classes with us for the next 2.5 years, but we also send you the box set with the CDs, DVDs, manuals, hard copies, etc. if you want to do it from home or online.

CLOSER: Now, do you see where it says "The System" to the right? That is our online library of everything you need to do this business effectively. This is where the nuts and bolts are, all the contracts, forms, how to videos, it's over 100 hours of content and we are always expanding it to add more tools for our students to use. Anything you ever need will be in THE SYSTEM and the system comes with 1 year of online group coaching with Stefan and all the students so once a month you have a group coaching session to see what other students are asking, so you essentially have two coaches, your accountability coach and Stefan your group coach.

CLOSER: Does it all of this make sense to you so far _____?

BUYER: Makes sense.

CLOSER: Okay, so let's talk about the result and the guarantee. The projected result that most students achieve by joining the Platinum program is completing twelve deals in a twelve to eighteen month timeframe. We worked it out earlier that the average deal in your market was worth $300,000 and you would net about 10 percent of the sale price in profit, do you follow?

BUYER: Yes.

CLOSER: So that leaves how much per deal for you?

BUYER: $30,000

CLOSER: Fantastic, okay, so if you made $30,000 a deal and did 12 deals, that would be $360,000 of profit, right? Okay, great, now let's talk about the tuition. The tuition for the Platinum program is—grab a pen and write this down—<<pause>> Okay, so I want you to write 12 x $30,000 =

$360,000, got it? Now below that, the tuition for the platinum is $72,000. But, what we have found in the past, _____, is that our best students are able to make decisions fairly quickly and move ahead with a contract and a deposit on a VISA or MASTERCARD, so if you move ahead today with a deposit to reserve your pricing and place in the program, it's only $60,000.

BUYER: ...

CLOSER: So _____, we're looking at a $60,000 investment to make $360,000 over the next twelve to eighteen months. Do you like the value; do you like the idea?

BUYER: Yeah of course, but OBJECTION ONE.

CLOSER: Yeah, I understand. Typically people who like the value and like the idea move ahead with a small deposit on a Visa or MasterCard to reserve their pricing and place in the program. We can take partial deposit today and work out the financing. Would you want to make that deposit on a VISA or MASTERCARD?

BUYER: 1st REAL OBJECTION TO BE DEFLECTED, ENTER CLOSING PROCESS.

PART THREE

THE CLOSE—7 LEVEL CLOSING—THE 7 LEVEL
LOCKDOWN SEQUENCE—7 LEVELS DOWN

The Closing Process

What does it mean "to close"? To close is to simply ask for the business directly. Simply ask for the money: ask the buyer to buy, and you will find out if he really likes your product or service or not. The customers who say "great presentation," "great information," "I really liked it" but didn't buy in reality didn't actually appreciate your offer enough to take it.

There is a story about two salesmen sitting on the curb, defeated after a long day of selling and one of them says to the other one, "I did some great presentations today."

The other one looks at him and says, "I didn't close anything either."

If you believe in your product or service, if you own your product or service, it is your ethical duty to deliver it to everyone who is qualified to solve their problem with it.

When you meet a prospect who has a problem and you fail to sell him on your offer, you have done him a disservice because 1) He didn't get his problem solved, 2) you wasted his time and yours, and 3) he is now going to go to the next competitor and buy something potentially inferior to your offer, and this is your fault because you didn't communicate the value well enough and didn't close him.

In the hit Disney movie *The Little Mermaid*, there is a famous song called "Kiss the Girl" in which the Little Mermaid and Prince Eric are in a small rowboat on date, and Sebastian the talking crab begins to sing "Kiss the Girl" to tempt Eric to kiss Ariel and lift the curse upon her soul.

Your prospect is like Ariel the Little Mermaid, and you are Prince Eric. She has a problem, a curse upon her soul, and when you are meeting her on your "sales date" if things go well, you will close and "kiss the girl." Just like a date, there is a perfect moment when a kiss could happen. In this perfect moment, if you go in for the kiss, or the close, you can fix and help your client's problem or curse. If you go in for the kiss too early, then you are violating her and could be accused of sexual assault. If you go in for the kiss or the close too late, then she doesn't feel pretty and is wondering why you hesitated.

The nature of sales is like the natural world of dating. To close is to find the perfect moment to "kiss the girl" and lift her curse.

A shockingly high percentage of professional salespeople make presentations without ever asking for the business. Many salespeople don't close, because they simply don't ask.

Sales is the only job in the world where you can do 99 percent of the work, presenting, traveling, prospecting, and following up, but if you don't close, you get 0 percent of the money.

In sales it's 100 percent or 0 percent, you are either the Rainmaking God in the office who makes it shower money whenever you walk in the door, or you are the dirt beneath management's feet.

Everybody Is on Commission

In truth, everyone, regardless of their job, base pay, salary, benefits, commissions, incentives, etc. is on commission. If you don't do the prescribed amount of work, you get fired.

If you work at McDonalds and only cook half the hamburger, you are fired.

The same works in sales; if you half bake the sale enough times you will be fired, and either you will run out of money to live on, or the company you work for will make room for someone who actually produces.

This book is called *The Close: 7 Level Selling* because closing is the result that everyone wants from selling. No one wants to sell; everyone wants to close. Closing is where you get paid, the company gets paid, the customer gets served, and the economy goes into motion. If you let the customer down, the customer doesn't get served, you don't get paid, the company doesn't get paid, and no one goes to work in the economy. Salespeople are heroes who put entire economies into motion and without them, there would be no prosperity.

The Three Tens
As identified by Jordan Belfort

In order for a customer to buy, he must believe in the three 10's: Your offer is a 10/10, You as a salesperson are 10/10 and the company you work for (doing the delivery) is a 10/10.

A 10 means that he thinks you are the best thing since sliced bread, a 5 is he's uncertain but likely closable, and 1 means that he thinks you are crap.

Whenever someone is not buying it's because they have not reached10 in all three categories, and it is your job to get them there.

Most objections people give you are nonsense; they do want to buy, but they feel uncertain about the offer, you, or the company.

Statistically speaking most sales are not made at the end of a presentation without resistance. True buyers have real money and real time at risk and will always put up some resistance before buying.

nexperienced closers will give up after one to three objections and let the prospect go.

Professional closers will drill down on the key issues and will circle the buyer at least five to seven times, which studies show is the effective amount of closes before winning the business.

Using the 7 level lockdown system below, many of the objections are handled before they happen so we will only loop a maximum of three times around, but you can loop as many times as necessary. You don't want to be perceived as a high pressure salesperson so three loops should be enough if you follow the system.

The 7 Level Closing Process

The 7 Level Closing Process works because all objections are the same. The buyer has uncertainty somewhere in the three 10s; they have a high action threshold, or they are not put into enough pain. The 7 Level Process is inspired by Jordan Belfort's Straight Line Closing Process, which, through my own study of that process, I was able to put my own natural closing practices into words. As a natural closer, I was performing several advanced sequences on my own, but until I studied Belfort, I was unable to put them into words to teach other people. The 7 Level Closing process follows the same language patterns and frameworks as the 7 Level Opening Process : Clichés, facts, opinions, hopes and dreams, feelings, fears/weaknesses, and needs. By using the 7 level opening, 7 level presentation and 7 level closing you will have ran the prospect through the 7 levels three times giving you an opportunity to use their familiar language patterns and have control throughout the entire sale until the close.

The 7 Level Closing Process, when executed properly, will run the buyer through at least 7 objections and will prevent novices from giving up too easily.

When to stop the 7 Level Process is if the prospect repeats the same objection two times in a row *or* has a change in demeanor, such as starting to laugh. Then it's time to go to level 7, the cutoff line, and set an appointment if there is interest or simply say, "How can I help you in the meantime?" and let the prospect reach back out to you, which means you lost the sale because buyers rarely reach out again *ever*. If the buyer is legit, you can set a future meeting.

Cracking the Code of Their Buying Strategy

The buyer will never tell you what their buying strategy is. In the questioning period you may uncover things like, "Have you made a purchase like this before?" or "How have you made decisions like this in the past?" and you may get some clues, but each buyer is a five digit combination lock, and you need to crack each digit one at a time to get the lock to open.

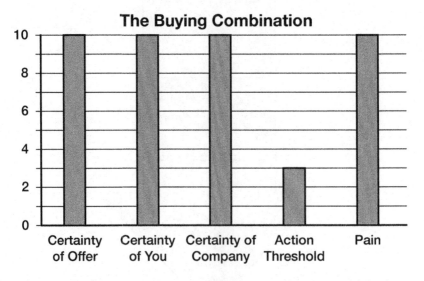

The buying combination is a 10–10–10–3–10 combination with high certainty on the offer, on you, on your company, a 3 on the action threshold, and a 10 on pain. This buyer will buy every time if he is in this combination. Certainty and pain must be higher than the action threshold.

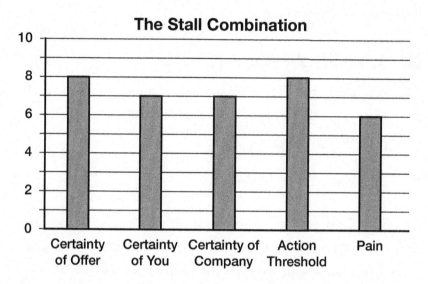

** Certainty must be higher than the action threshold to close

What happens more often than not is a stall where the buyer is something like an 8–7–7–8–6 where his certainty is not high enough for him to move forward, and his action threshold is too high, so he will throw up a smokescreen or a stall to avoid moving forward. Humans want to avoid uncertainty at all costs, so this is a natural defense.

The only way to pick the lock is to methodically go through each piece:

3. Certainty in your offer
4. Certainty in you and your belief systems
5. Certainty in your brand and belief systems
6. Lower the action threshold
7. Increase the pain threshold

One at a time and slowly, change the numbers to the right combination to win the sale. Rather than fumbling around in the dark trying to find the "real objection" or giving up after one or two objections like novice sales people in a rapport-destroying death spiral that breaks all agreement, you are much better off taking a methodical approach towards handling each digit of the lock one at a time.

Live Action Script—Closing

CLOSER: So the projected result you will see from doing twelve deals in a year at roughly $30,000 of profit per deal is $360,000 net profit to you; is that too much money for you, _____?

BUYER: No, no, it's not (laughs).

CLOSER: Okay great, now, the tuition for the Platinum, I want you to write this down . . . The program is typically $72,000 but if we move ahead today on the phone with a contract and a deposit, it's only $60,000 . . .

<<silence>>

CLOSER: So $60,000 should get you around $360,000 in twelve to eighteen months if you follow the program and do the twelve deals that you set out to do. Do you like the value? Do you like the idea?

BUYER: Yeah, I do like the idea.

CLOSER: Okay great. Typically people who like the value and like the idea move ahead with a deposit on a VISA or a MASTERCARD to reserve their pricing and their place in the program; which would be better for you today, _____? VISA or MASTERCARD?

BUYER: Let me think about it and get back to you.

LEVEL 1 Cliché—Deflect the Token Objection

The first objection is hardly ever the real objection; simply deflect it with a trial close: "Does the idea make sense to you?" or "Do you like the idea?" to disable it and move on to the real objections. The first objection is Cliché and often meaningless.

CLOSER: I hear what you are saying, _____. Let me ask you a question: Does the idea make sense to you? Do you like the idea? (money aside tonality)

LEVEL 2 Resell The Fact That They Like The Offer

Level 2 is about reinforcing the fact that they do like the value and the idea, this is a fact that you need to test for validity and get them to a 10/10 on enthusiasm for your offer.

BUYER: Yeah, I guess it's okay.

DECIDE: *(Gauge the level of certainty in the product 1–10) Enthusiasm means a 10, 1 is utter disgust, 5 or a 6 is positive and can be closed. You will need to loop around and resell the product. If he's a 5 or 6 do not ask for the close, he's not certain enough. Pick up where the logical case of the presentation left off and frame the product airtight logically and emotionally.*

CLOSER: Exactly! It really is a great buy here! In fact, one of the true beautifies of the program is . . . RESELL THE KEY POINTS THEY LIKED

CLOSE OUT PATTERN: You see what I'm saying here, _____ ? Do you like the idea?

BUYER: Yes! I see it

Enthusiastic yes = 8, ready to move onto the next piece

If the buyer responds below a 3 enthusiasm, end the encounter; they aren't a real buyer

If the buyer is below a 2 in enthusiasm, repeat his answer back to him in an incredulous tone, challenge him to get him to an 8

LEVEL 3 Opinions—Resell You And Your Belief Systems

CLOSER: Pause (mystery and intrigue tone) Now, _____, let me ask you another question . . . (money aside tone) If I had been your strategist for the last three or four years making you money on a consistent basis (switch tone to implied obviousness) then you probably wouldn't be saying, "Let me think about it right now, _____" You'd be saying, "Get me started with the next program!" (switch to reasonable man tone) Am I right?

BUYER: Yeah, well, then I would . . . OR Obviously! I mean, who wouldn't want that right?

(This admits that trust or lack of trust in you is the cornerstone issue 5 percent of prospects fit into this category)

CLOSER: (mocking tone mixed with incredulous tone) Wait a second, _____, you mean to tell me that if I put you into the Bronze program at $18,000 and made you $30,000 , and I put you in the Silver program for $30,000 and made you $90,000 and put you in the Gold at $40,000 and made you $180,000, then you wouldn't be saying, "Get me started with the Platinum program" right now, on the spot, come on?

BUYER: Yeah, well, in THAT case I would *(slightly defensive as if it wasn't their fault for flip flopping on the answer; it was your fault for flip flopping on the*

question. They have been called out on their bullshit, and now they are trying to backpedal and save face. This avoids the stupid counter, "What's there to think about?" That is a dead-end question and will threaten his mind and break rapport. The real objection is he doesn't know you and therefore has no basis for trusting you and you brought that to light in a very elegant way without threatening him. You now have sixty seconds to sell yourself and build trust.)

CLOSER: (sympathy tone) Now, *that* I can understand. You don't know me and I don't have the luxury of a track record; so let me take a moment to reintroduce myself.

CLOSER: My name is [YOUR FIRST AND LAST NAME], and I'm a [YOUR TITLE] at the [NAME OF YOUR COMPANY], and I've been there for [ACTUAL NUMBER] years and I pride myself on . . . (tell them a little bit about yourself citing):

- ✓ Degrees
- ✓ Licenses
- ✓ Special talents
- ✓ Awards you've won
- ✓ What your goals are with the company
- ✓ Where you stand in terms of ethics, integrity and customer service. These are the belief systems that the customer wants to tap into.
- ✓ How you can be an asset to him and his family over the long term. A long term relationship with you is a major asset to the customer going forward especially if you sell your belief systems strongly.

NOTE: *Also create a secondary version of yourself and a tertiary version of yourself so you can loop and resell as you need if the sale drags on and you need to talk about yourself intelligently.*

LEVEL 4 Hopes and Dreams—Resell The Brand
Based On Belief Systems of the Company
You have finished selling yourself and now transition into reselling the company with the transition, "As far as the brand XYZ goes . . ."

CLOSER: Now only am I going to guide you into the idea, but I'm going to guide you out as well. As far as the brand, [XYZ COMPANY] goes, it's one of the most respected . . ."

- ✓ We stand for X belief system
- ✓ We are #1 in this
- ✓ We're the fastest growing that
- ✓ We're the foremost experts in this
- ✓ The chairman of the board, a man named so and so has one of the most astute minds in the ABC industry
- ✓ He's accomplished X
- ✓ He's accomplished Y
- ✓ And he's built this company around one thing above all: [WHATEVER THAT IS]

CLOSER: (complete the pattern with) So, _____, why don't we do this . . . OR all I'm asking for is . . . *(then transition into the close, or if allowed, try to downsell them a bit to dip their toe and get started with something small; after they've seen what a great job you do, you can work on a much higher level)*

- ✓ If you give me 1 percent of your trust, I'll earn the other 99 percent
- ✓ Frankly, on such a small sale like this, after I split my commission with the firm and the government, I can't put puppy chow in my dog's bowl.
- ✓ I'm obviously not getting rich here, but, again, this will serve as a benchmark for future business.

People with low action thresholds will start to close here. 20 percent will close right here.

You may need to run additional loops to:

1. Increase their level of certainty for one or more of the three tens
2. Lowering their action threshold
3. Increasing their pain threshold

LEVEL 5 Feelings—"how's it going to feel?"
Lower the action threshold

If the buyer isn't closed, he is now going to objection-hop and suddenly need to "talk to their wife or accountant" or "send me an email or some information" or "it's a bad time of year"

Most salespeople hit with one objection have a problem handling it; getting hit with two objections is overwhelming.

Most salespeople are trained to handle the first objection with a canned response to an objection which is fake or a smokescreen, and then re-ask for the order. The first objection is usually a smokescreen so the salesperson wasted his time and energy handling a non-objection.

You cannot deflect the second objection, as it would look too evasive and would break trust.

The Action Threshold

The brain runs two separate movies through the mind: a positive one and a negative one. The positive one is filled with all the benefits and wonderful things that will happen if the product turns out to as great as it was sold. The negative movie contains all the downside risk, painful things you'll experience in the future if it turns out that the salesman misled you and the product is garbage. What's the best case? And what's the worst case?

A person with a high action threshold has a beautiful positive movie that is much stronger in their mind, and a person with a low action threshold has a negative movie that is much stronger in their mind. The threshold is determined by which movie is dominant.

A person with a low action threshold can be 7–8–7 on the certainty scale and a person with a high action threshold will need 10–10–10 to buy.

Four Ways to Lower the Action Threshold

1. Money-back guarantee
2. A cooling off rescission period also known as cancellation period of X number of days
3. Key phrases and promises: "I'll hold your hand every step of the way" "We pride ourselves on long term relationships," or "We have world-class customer service."
4. Temporarily reverse the parallel movies in their mind, get them to abandon the long intense negative movie and enjoy the positive one.

CLOSER: (agree with the objection) loop around to version 2 of "you" and version 2 of "the company"

Resell You in Way #2
✓ Your belief systems about why you are in business
✓ Degrees
✓ Licenses
✓ Special talents
✓ Awards you've won
✓ What your goals are with the company
✓ Where you stand in terms of ethics, integrity and customer service
✓ How you can be an asset to him and his family over the long term

Resell The Brand in Way #2

✓ We stand for X belief system.

✓ We are #1 in this

✓ We're the fastest growing that

✓ We're the foremost experts in this

✓ The chairman of the board, a man named so and so has one of the most astute minds in the ABC industry

✓ He's accomplished X

✓ He's accomplished Y

✓ And he's built this company around one thing above all: [WHATEVER THAT IS]

CLOSER: _____, let me ask you an honest question: what's the worst that can possibly happen here? I mean, let's say I'm wrong and the program is only half as good as I say it is and you end up losing a few thousand bucks: is that going to put you in the poorhouse?"

BUYER: No (begrudgingly).

CLOSER: Exactly: of course it won't! And, on the upside, let's say I'm right—like we both think I am—the program works as well for you as it has for so many other people and you make only a hundred grand in real estate. I mean, it'll feel good and everything, but it's not going to make you the richest man in town, now, will it?

BUYER: No, definitely not.

CLOSER: Exactly! Of course it won't. It's not going to make you rich, and it's not going to make you poor, but what this program will do is serve as benchmark for future business. It'll show you that I know how to put you into the right program at the right time and get you the results you want. So why don't we do this: since this is our first time working together, why don't we start off a bit smaller this time. Instead of picking up the Platinum program, let's pick up the Gold instead, which is cash outlay of only $40,000. Of course, you'll make a bit less money as it's a shorter program and you won't get as much done, but your percentage gain remains the same, and you can judge me on that alone; and believe me, _____, if you only do even half as well as the rest of my clients in this program, the only problem you're going to have is that you didn't buy more. *Sound fair enough?"* [then shut up and wait for a response]

NOTE: If you stay quiet, 75 percent of prospects will buy right here. If you close the high action threshold prospect, you have earned a prize because these people are loyal for life to a salesperson and will pay more for you just because they like you to avoid risk from other companies.

LEVEL 6 Fears and Weaknesses—Increase the Pain Threshold

People who are feeling significant pain tend to act quickly while people in denial of their pain act slowly.

Introduce pain in the questioning and intelligence gathering phase in level 6 and in the third loop. You can play off the pain during the presentation and use it for perspective.

Two Ways to Put the Buyer in Pain

1. They are already in pain from a life occurrence
2. Language patterns

CLOSER: (re-introduce the buyer's pain from level 6 of the questioning period) Now, _____, I know you said before that you're worried about your retirement in terms of having nothing to fall back on . . . (and so forth.) What do you think is going to happen to your situation if you fail to take action to fix it?

CLOSER: (empathetic tone) _____, let me ask you a question: given how things have been deteriorating over the last twelve months, where do you see yourself in a year from now? Or, even worse, five years from now? Are things going to be even more intense, in terms of all the sleepless nights and the worrying?" *(maintain sympathetic tone throughout the pattern)*

BUYER: I'll be in the same spot I'm in now, but probably a lot worse.

CLOSER: *(I feel your pain tone)* I get it, _____. I've been around the block a couple thousand times now, and I know that these things typically don't resolve themselves unless *you* take serious action to resolve them.

CLOSER: In fact, let me say this: one of the true beauties here is that . . . *(resell the 3 tens in the short concise tertiary pattern focusing almost exclusively on the emotional side of the equation. Then future pace him into what his life is going to look and feel great after he receives the exact benefits he was promised and from the emotional high, transition into the soft close ask for the order again.)*

Resell You in an Emotional Way

✓ Your belief systems on why you are in business

✓ Degrees

✓ Licenses

✓ Special Talents

✓ Awards you've won

✓ What your goals are with the company

✓ Where you stand in terms of ethics, integrity and customer service

✓ How you can be an asset to him and his family over the long term

Resell The Company in an Emotional Way

✓ Your brand's belief systems especially on customer service

✓ We are #1 in this

✓ We're the fastest growing that

✓ We're the foremost experts in this

✓ The chairman of the board, a man named so and so has one of the most astute minds in the ABC industry

✓ He's accomplished X

✓ He's accomplished Y

✓ And he's built this company around one thing above all: [WHATEVER THAT IS]

LEVEL 7 Needs—"How can I help you in the meantime?" THE CUTOFF

If the buyer repeats the same objection again two times in a row, thank him for his time to avoid being a high-pressure salesman looping him to death. Have intuitive sales ability.

If your prospect's demeanor changes, by laughing or getting edgy, it's because they feel pressured and you have gone too far.

CLOSER: _____, please don't misconstrue my enthusiasm for pressure; it's just that I know that this is *truly* a perfect fit for you (two options follow):

OPTION 1: Loop back around into the sale one more time and give it one more shot, paying close attention to the tonality and body language of your prospect. If they are showing interest, and buying body language then continue; if not, continue to option 2

OPTION 2: Second meeting

CLOSER: _____, please don't misconstrue my enthusiasm for pressure; it's just that I know this is truly is a perfect fit for you (tone of utter sincerity). So why don't we do this: let me send you the information you are looking for (or whatever the last objection was) and give you a few days to look through everything and also discuss it with your wife, and then we can set a time next week to speak again once you've had a chance to really get your arms wrapped around everything. Sound good?

DECIDE: Set the meeting if they are serious, or let them call you back and give them your number if they aren't. A great way to end a non-sale or a stall is "How can I help you in the meantime?" this implies that you are here to fill their needs, whether you can or not.

The Line of Money, Upsells and Downsells

At the time of the close and once the sale has been made, you have brought the prospect over the line of money, and he is now a customer. Turn him into a client (a repeat customer) by offering upsells, bundles and downsells.

Once the client is over the line of money, he is seven times easier to close than someone who has never given you or your company money. That could be because he already knows you, knows your company, has a track record, trusts you, and really it just comes down to the new product and new offer and whether it make sense for him.

In the 7 level closing sequence, we started at the bigger offer that would totally fill the client's needs and went for the downsell to "test the waters" and earn the relationship. You may not want to rock the boat if the client is still a little uneasy or uncertain, but if the sale was easier and on a low action threshold individual then you can try.

"Hey, I almost forgot, we just came out with this new program. It does XYZ benefit in ABC Result in Q Time, it goes great with the package you just purchased, and it's only $797. Should I write it up in the order now too?" You typically want to do this after all the payment details have already been written down and you can simply say, "I'll just change the charge on the card by a few digits and put it in the order."

When people are finally making purchase is when they feel best about you, your product, and your company, so the moment of "crossing the money line" is a magical moment where you can really maximize sales and profits with almost zero extra effort.

Nested Loops

When making an upsell you may want to enter into a nested loop pattern where a loop represents an idea or a pitch you are offering. You have already made the sale, and now you are opening three additional loops with other offers.

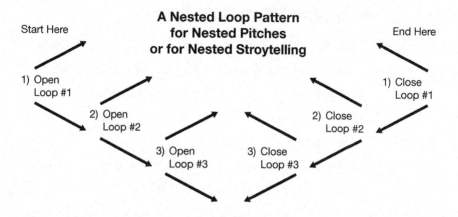

Loop #1 opens with your first upsell "By the way, I wanted to tell you about our XYZ program, I know it might not be for you, but it's on special, and if I didn't mention it to you and you found out later, you would be mad . . ." followed by a short presentation and a soft close: "Should I add that into your order?" You may open to enter a second pitch or loop with Loop #2 "By the way, most people who purchased the package you have today typically add on this complimentary product. . . ." Whether you are successful with the second Loop, you may enter a third looping pattern: "Hey, I almost forgot . . ." with a third upsell and another offer.

Once you have opened your nested loops, you must then close them out in reverse sequence from Loop #3 to Loop #2 to Loop#1 to have the highest chance of success in upselling multiple sales on one call.

These loops are best closed with soft closes instead of hard closes as you are simply taking the easiest and most natural "second" and "third" money available and offering easy natural complimentary offers.

You can open a multiple loop sequence with storytelling, which can be powerful in presenting or objection handling. Nested loops are an advanced technique to present multiple ideas, stories, and offers to the human mind, which can typically only operate with one idea at a time.

The Counterintuitive Nature of the Upsell

If you are having objections about the price, for example, or maybe you are pitching a lower priced program $1,000 item with a lower result, or something too entry level to someone who is too high level, they will object on price. The answer to this objection is to offer him a high value offer at $50,000 that might actually fit his needs.

You will see this often with consulting firms where they offer a lower price "do it yourself package for $1,000 to $3,000" and often the real high ticket buyers won't even bother because they want a much better, white glove service. Do not be afraid to go on a mega upsell if price becomes the sticking point and the buyer is a little more sophisticated.

A good rule of thumb is to size the product to his ego and what he thinks of himself and his company so that you can bring something relevant to the table.

Stock Closes

Although I'm a firm believer in highly precise language and execution through polished scripts for every sales presentation, there is value to having a collection of standard closes at your fingertips. They may be useful to try experimentally or in situations where the script isn't quite dialed in yet.

The major problem with stock closes is that they can be executed unpracticed, and some of them are pure nonsense. There are books out there containing 100+ closes and novice salespeople can get drunk on the Kool-Aid idea of memorizing a bunch of nonsensical closes out of context.

Novice salespeople will go into a rapport-building death spiral answering objection after objection and either 1) give up after two or three attempts or 2) start to turn off the client and turn the close into an argument. You always want to close as elegantly as possible to avoid those two common mistakes.

Besides systematically locking down on closes by having an airtight script and process, a good method for keeping in your back pocket is this:

Standard Objection Isolation Process

1. Feed it back (followed by a pause)
2. Acknowledge the objection, agree
3. Besides this, would there be any other reason to not move ahead today?
   Get the new objection (loop that sequence until you get down to the core issue)
4. Get commitment on the objection, "If I could show you a way to afford it today, would you move ahead?"
5. Defeat the objection
6. Pattern interrupt
7. Close

Standard Objection Isolation Process
Live Action Example

CLIENT: Yeah, sounds good, let me think about and get back to you.

1. **Feed it back (followed by a pause)—slowly with pause and**

CLOSER: " . . . Think about it and get back to me?"

CLIENT: Yeah . . . I'll get back to you

CLOSER: . . . (pause to wait to see if the silence changes their mind)

Note: This first move is to test the validity of their knee-jerk objection, which is similar to a deflection. Often when the client hears the absurd nature of their own words, they sometimes retract or refute the objection.

2. **Acknowledge the objection, agree–**

CLOSER: "I understand, John. Sometimes I feel like I need to think about things too, but let me ask you this":

3. **Besides this, would there be any other reason to not move ahead today?**
   a. ****Get the new objection (loop that sequence until you get down to the core issue)****

CLOSER: "Besides wanting to think about it, would there be any other reason to not move ahead today?"

CLIENT: "Well, I haven't spoken to my wife... we make decisions together."

CLOSER: "Mmmhmm, and besides that would there be any other reason stopping you from moving ahead today?"

CLIENT: "I'm not sure if I can afford it. I don't have $10,000 cash today!"

CLOSER: "Okay and besides the cash would there be anything else stopping you from moving ahead today?

CLIENT: "No, that's it; my wife is concerned about the cash. I don't want her to think I was making decisions without her."

4. **Get commitment on the objection, "If I could show you a way to afford it today, would you move ahead?"**

CLOSER: "I understand, John; so the cash is the main issue then?"

CLIENT: "Yeah, we don't have it.

CLOSER: "I can understand that; not everyone who works with our company has all of the cash upfront; in fact, most of them don't. If I could show you way to afford it today would you move ahead?"

CLIENT: Sure, how?

5. **Defeat the objection (show financing program for dollars a day vs. big cash up front)**

CLOSER: "I'm glad you asked, John. I completely understand your situation. Using our in-house financing, I can get that cash outlay reduced to $0 out of pocket and installments of only $79 a month, which really *anyone* can afford . . ."

6. **Pattern Interrupt**—Before you ask for the business you can break their mental thought process by asking an unrelated question to get their mind off the sale.

CLOSER: "What did you have for breakfast yesterday, John?"

CLIENT: "Eggs."

7. **Close**—Now you follow up by defeating the true objection once and for all, in this case; financing breaks the product down into smaller monthly payments.

CLOSE: "Fantastic, all you have to do is fill out this short application, and I can get this product to delivered within the week,; let's get started."

CLIENT: Okay. Lets do it.

Standard Closes

The following is a list of standard sales closes that are used in a variety of environments to close the deal. There are literally hundreds of closes but you should get to know and memorize a few basic ways to ask for the business, especially if you are suddenly caught without a script.

Puppy dog close—"Why don't you take it home today John and give it a try. Keep it for a week, and if you don't like it, bring it back at no cost to you."

This close was supposedly used in pet shops to sell puppy dogs. Apparently no one ever had the heart to return a puppy after having him for a week. If your product or service allows this sort of trial period, this could be gold.

Ben Franklin close—"Those are excellent points you make John. Let's grab a piece of paper and write down all of the reasons why we should do this and all of the reasons why not to do this and once you see it on a piece of paper, you can decide."

This was supposedly a way that Ben Franklin made decisions by writing all the pros and cons on a piece of paper and weighing it out. If you have done a good sales presentation you should have several reasons why to move ahead and very few to not move ahead.

Sharp angle close—"I hear you, John: you don't have the money. The reason why you don't have the money today is because you didn't do something like this five years ago. How long are you going to put this off? Let make this happen for you."

Paradoxically, the reason *not* to buy is also the reason to buy.

"I don't have any time" becomes
"You would have more time if you took the program."

"I don't have any money" becomes
"You would have more money if you took the program."

"I can't do it because I have kids" becomes "I must do it because I have kids."

Walk away, take away, today only close—"Well, John, I'm sorry; it sounds like this offer just isn't for you . . . It's okay; it's not for everyone" (slowly start to pack your bags and do a slow walk to the door and the car. "Unfortunately, this offer is only available today on the first-call special is company policy, and if you want it, I can get you started right now, and if not, the offer expires . . ." (Slowly walk away)

This is a hard closing technique that should only be used sparingly because it can make egos flare and damage your relationship with the other side.

Invitational close—(Preceded by a trial close) "Do you like the idea so far?" or "Does what I have shown you make sense to you?" (Followed by a "yes" from the customer.) You then say, "If you like what I have shown you, why don't you give it a try?"

This is a softer more classy close than others.

Directive close (the next step is)—"Well, John, it sounds like you like the value and like the idea, so the next step would be to get started with the paperwork, and I should be able to have the service delivered by Monday as we discussed."

This is a very popular close in a wide variety of industries.

Preferential close (A or B)—"Fantastic, John. I'm glad you like the value and like the idea, would you like to get started with a Visa or a MasterCard today?"

This is a very common binary close and takes the buyer away from the yes or no binary of "Should I buy this or not?"

Incremental close (wood crate vs. cardboard)—"Mr. Prospect, I know you haven't decided to make an order yet, but if you were to order, would you prefer your product delivered in a wood crate or a cardboard crate?"

Another variation is, "Fantastic, what is the best zip/postal code to ship the product to?"

These are small closes to use incrementally to gain commitment before going for the big close.

Authorization close—"Do you have any further questions or concerns, Mr. Prospect?" The prospect does not, so you grab the contract, check off the boxes, and push it towards him with a pen ready to sign and say, "Well then, if you will just authorize this, we will get started right away."

This is used in very large multimillion dollar deals.

Ultimatum close—You and the prospect have been going back and forth for some time now with multiple meetings, and the sale is starting to waste your time and his.

You say, "Mr. Prospect, I know how busy you are; we've been talking about this product for some time now, and either this is a good idea for you, or it isn't. If it's a good idea, we should make the decision right now and get on with it. If not, your time is too valuable to continue talking about it. If you will authorize this, we'll get started right away."

Reserve the Ultimatum for the last resort when it comes to closing, and typically you can avoid this by setting a meeting limit up front with your prospect: "Mr. Prospect, I understand you want to have a second meeting and that is no problem, but usually most people are able to make a decision in two meetings, so if you can, please have everything you need ready to make a firm decision."

When setting the third meeting: "Okay, Mr. Prospect, I'll set a third meeting with you so you can sort out XYZ details, but I want to let you know that I never book a fourth meeting. Either this is for you on the third meeting, or it's not. I don't want to waste your time."

Order sheet close—At the end of your presentation take out your order sheet and begin to fill it out, look down at the paperwork with your pen and say, "What's the correct spelling of your first and last name, Mr. Prospect?"

It can be aggressive to pull out the order form earlier, and start filling out the terms and delivery date during the presentation as well. You will have to go with your gut as to whether you can pull this off one on one. In real estate sales I have found it to be very effective.

Some sales organizations instruct their sales people to fill out the paperwork in the car in advance to psych themselves up and visualize the prospect's order coming through. This can be a very powerful technique.

"I want to think it over" close—The prospect responds "I have to think about it . . ."

You respond, smiling. "Mr. Prospect, that's a good idea. This is an important decision, and I don't want you to rush into anything."

The client will relax because he thinks the sale is over

Then you ask in a curious tone "Mr. Prospect, obviously you have good reason for wanting to think it over, so may I ask what it is? Is it the money?"

Hard Closing vs. Soft Closing

When you are closing you are asking for the business and as a professional salesperson you need to become a master of both Hard Closing and Soft Closing. There are times where you can elegantly soft close the client into the product or service and there is a low percentage chance that he is a laydown and easy business.

Soft closes are soft, easy, pillowy, light ways of asking for the business. Unskilled salespeople usually only practice a few soft easy closes and then walk away with discomfort. On the other end of the spectrum is the master closer who is so elegant in his delivery that he is able to drill down on the key issues in a soft way—like a ninja master—and keep the rapport intact the whole time. An example would be using the 7 Level Lockdown System where the entire process is scripted, manicured, and polished into the cleanest script possible. The 7 level closing script only handles three real objections but subtly handles much more in a subtle, elegant, methodical way.

However, there are times when a hard close is necessary. A hard close is where "things get hard" and the rapport gets strained or can even break. A hard closer can sit through six, seven, or eight objections and is committed to sitting until the deal is done. You've got to prepare yourself mentally for this the way an Olympic athlete would prepare himself physically.

In many ways, a hard close is much more of a negotiation than a sale, and that is why I believe all salespeople should become astute students of negotiation as well as sales. Sales allows you to present and sell well, build value, and be elegant, whereas negotiation is down-and-dirty slugging in the trenches. If sales were a Formula 1 Race car flying down a straight path on pure octane and fuel—an efficient machine, negotiation would be a rusty old monster truck, chugging diesel and slogging it out in the mud.

Personally I come from a background of buying distressed real estate on the street and coaching people to break down their belief systems and change their lives, often taking on more financial risk than they ever have before. Both of those can require hard closing skills, so I am okay with sitting through a seven objection hard close as long or as hard as it takes because I know my product or service is true and right for the customer. There may be tears, there may be crying, there may be moments of severe despair, I even had a client sign up for my program, his wife threatened to divorce him, he called in for a refund, and I said, "Does she support you in your endeavors?" He said "no," and I said, "She's not your wife." They got divorced; my client changed his life and became successful afterwards, but the remedy for the darkness of hard closing is having a high belief in service and to deeply care about the customer.

If you are doing what is right, you can put up with an unbearable amount of pain.

In sales, you can only close as hard as you care. As Zig Ziglar said, "They don't care about how much you know until they know how much you care."

Having strong ethics, a strong, almost religious faith, or zealous like belief in your mission and serving the greater good can make you able to deal with the most difficult closes of all and sit through life-changing moments.

Some salespeople are against the hard close. I think it's something you need to develop a thick skin to and keep it in your repertoire because the biggest and hardest deals sometimes cannot be closed with elegance and must be closed in a hard way.

The Power of Silence

The roar of silence is one of the most powerful closing tools around. We have two ears and one mouth to use in the exact proportion 2:1, so listen twice as much as you talk. Silence is very powerful when closing because it allows you to "shut up and listen" to what the prospect is saying, and you become highly perceptive to his breathing, body language, and other subtle cues.

It's a common myth that extroverts make better salespeople than introverts, but in truth, a trained introvert has a massive advantage over his bumbling extroverted counterpart. Extroverts will talk, and talk, and talk, and talk themselves out of a sale, whereas an introvert will sit there and listen until the prospect is finished.

Remember the conscious mind operates at 500 words per minute while you can only speak at 100–200 words per minute, so every time you plunge into silence, their mind begins to race, and as an untrained salesperson, so will yours.

I was recently training a group of young salespeople in a role play and performed my close and then waited in silence. Hardly ten seconds passed before the young salespeople started to giggle and snicker; they looked at each other and turned red in embarrassment. People are not used to pure silence, and when you can unleash that upon them, it can be a very powerful tool for applying pressure.

They say that the music isn't in the notes; it's the spaces in between the notes that make the music, which is also known as the silence.

Learn to calm your mind down and be able to sit perfectly still waiting in silence for your prospect to react, and typically the person who breaks the silence first loses.

Punctuate your speech with silence, use silence after asking for the business, and use it for dramatic effect in your presentations. You will be amazed at the power of silence.

Key issues—1 major, 3 minor issues

As with negotiation, in sales, there is usually one major issue for a buyer to object and three minor issues. One is a need and three are wants. You need to be able to establish the differences between what the buyer wants and what the buyer needs.

In the wise words of Henry Ford, "If I asked my customers what they wanted, they would have told me a faster horse."

Sometimes the customer doesn't really know what he wants, so you must give him what he needs.

As a salesperson you must drill down on the key issues in the questioning phase, and potentially the closing phase to determine what the key issue is so that you can solve it.

Buying Questions

Years ago in my very early twenties I saw an ad online that read "get government money for your business." I was twenty-one, young and naïve, and clicked the ad requesting some information. The next morning a phone salesman called me while I was in bed, barely awake. In fact, the phone woke me up. I answered the phone and on the other end was a salesman with a French accent from Montreal. Although he had a French accent, he sounded like a pro on the phone.

The reason for the call was that I requested some information and he was there to give it to me; he pitched me on his company, which compiled all of the grant information in the country and provided it to your door so that you could apply for as many grants as you wanted: you could get funding for your business, your family, your house, a new car, an entire myriad of government money—millions of dollars was waiting for me, if only I purchased his binder of compiled grant information.

"How much is it?" I asked

The salesman said "What's your postal code sir?"

I gave him my postal code and he closed me on a $300 binder of grant information that came promptly in the mail.

At the time I was amazed that this guy knew that I wanted to buy and was so slick and smooth about closing me.

Later had a job at a phone sales company and told my trainer about the French grant salesman who sold me as soon as I asked how much his program was and closed me by getting my postal code, increasing the commitment.

She said, "Of course, it's because you asked a buying question! It's a signal you were ready to buy."

She was right, and then I learned the power of buying questions.

Types of Buying Indicators

    a. Price and terms—"How much?" , "Are payment plans available?"

    b. More details—"I'd like to know more about the guarantee."

    c. Delivery—"When can you deliver the product by?"

d. Body language (chin touching or tea kettle)—Touching the chin usually signifies deep thought.

e. Calculating numbers—When the buyer starts breaking down the numbers, "So you are telling my for X dollars I get Y result? That works out to Z per transaction . . ."

f. Sudden friendliness—A change in positive demeanor towards you. "Hey, that looks great! Mike—can I call you Mike?"

Common Types of Objections

General sales resistance—A general aversion to salespeople and the sales process. They hate being sold but must buy at some point. All real customers with real money to spend have real general sales resistance, and they will put up at least one objection to avoid feeling like a "lay down." This is good, because people who are quick to buy are usually unqualified and have no money, so they have nothing to lose and will jump right in until you find out they have no money. As a salesperson you should welcome general buyer's resistance because it usually means the buyer is for real and has something to lose. If they act like they have no money, they actually could have quite a bit. People don't get rich by giving it away.

Requests for information—"I need more information" is is something you should welcome as a salesperson. Requests for information are good because they usually indicate interest, and if you can educate the buyer enough, they will buy.

Objective objections—"What proof do you have?" These are good objections as well; all you have to do is be able to back up your claims. Remember, they say it—it's real. When you say it, it's hearsay to be untrusted. Be prepared to back up your claims with case studies, testimonials, sources, and anything else to justify your proof of claims.

Subjective objections—Any type of objection about you, these seem to come from salespeople talking about themselves and their companies too much and can create a "I just don't like him" feeling. If you sense this happening, switch the focus onto the customer, which it should be on anyways.

Excuses—"I'm not in the market right now" or some shallow put-off to get rid of the salesperson. "I'm too busy for that right now" or "I don't like the color." Know that these are not real objections to a lack of interest; they are simply there to save the buyer time and energy.

Show-off objections—"I have a lot of experience in your industry" is the buyer puffing his chest for recognition, to be right and to be liked. Play into his need and make him feel superior: "Of course someone with your experience can see that X . . ."

Malicious objections—You may come across someone who is overly defensive and negative who says, "Salespeople are just out for a quick buck!" or "I've tried a service like yours before and I got ripped off!" or other negativity like that. These people have been burned in the past by a salesperson, and all you need to do is sympathize: "I understand exactly how you feel. If I were in your position I would feel the same way."

Unspoken objections—These objections are landmines because you will get your presentation 95 percent of the way to the close and the unspoken objection is stopping you. There is some uncertainty left in the buyer's mind about you, your offer or your company holding them back. Get them to 10 on the three 10s.

Time—Every buyer, whether it's a person or company, has a time constraint that they are dealing with. We all have twenty-four hours in a day, so this is mostly an excuse.

Money—If the buyer has some money and financing ability also known as the ability to get loans, money is never an issue. The only time money is an issue is if the buyer has literally no job, zero cash, bad credit and is pretty much a deadbeat. Even then, you can get a friend or family member to sponsor him into your offer. Money is never a real objection. The real objection is they feel uncertain about the three 10s.

Fear (uncertainty is a better word)—Replace the word "fear" in your vocabulary for "uncertainty" and you will look at fear in a whole new light. When you are fearful, it's an emotion, and you can't quite pinpoint what the fear is. Uncertainty is a feeling, where you ask yourself, "Uncertain about what?" Ultimately all objections are simply a lack of certainty and if you can increase the certainty in you, your offer, and your company, the buyer will buy.

Pride—"I don't think I need it. I'm better than that product" may be true or may not be. Usually this is pride talking, and all you have to ask is, "Why are you here then? Why haven't you got the result you really desire yet?" or "Why hasn't this happened for you yet?" To stop pride, you need a big dose of reality to balance the ego out.

All Objections Are the Same—Uncertainty

The remedy for all objections is certainty. The buyer must reach a state of certainty where he knows your product is a 10—the best thing since sliced bread—you are a 10 and the only choice of a person to be delivering it to him and servicing him, and your company is a 10—a great company to be proud of. In the end, all objections are the same, a form of uncertainty. When you begin to look at all objections being the same, you can begin to handle them in more methodical ways and really drill down on your mechanics of closing the deal instead of worrying about memorizing 100 different objections as so many salespeople attempt to do.

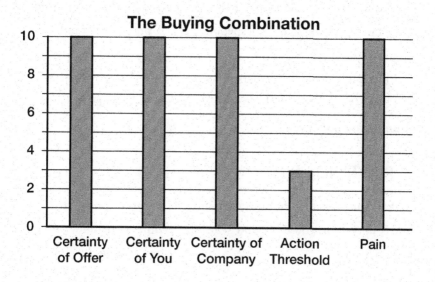

Asking for Referrals

As a business owner I know firsthand that marketing is a major expense for every business, and leads cost money, and so does general customer acquisition. Acquiring a new customer takes seven times the effort to acquire over reselling an old customer or asking for a referral, and in the old days they used to say that it takes seven exposures of advertising to win a customer.

Tony Robbins once delivered a business seminar and revealed a new number for 2017 and that was that it is now fourteen times exposure to get a new customer. Many companies spend anywhere from 14 percent to 33 percent of their top line revenue on customer acquisition alone! That money goes into marketing, advertising, travel, trade shows, and sometimes sales commissions, but usually just the costs to get the customer to say "Hello."

In my early twenties I worked in an inbound sales call center, and on the wall was a sign that said "IT COSTS $18 TO GET THE PHONE TO RING"! That business owner had to pay $18 just to get the phone to ring for an opportunity for one of his salespeople to do a presentation and make a commission!

With this being said, a salesperson who can get referrals from his existing client base is worth his weight in gold to the business owner. Referrals cost nothing—you just have to ask.

The Best Time to Ask

The best time to get a referral is right after the sale is made and the paperwork is drying on the table and you ask, "Before I go John, one quick question for you."

"Sure what is it?"

"About the product we got you started with today: what's the thing you loved most about it?"

"Oh, I love that it's going to get me the result in eight weeks, guaranteed!"

"Fantastic, who do you know that would also love getting the same result in eight weeks, guaranteed?"

This is a powerful way to ask for a testimonial because 1) he is in—he purchased and is invested, 2) we are asking for the thing loved the most and using the emotion he felt to see who else would like to feel that same way, and 3) the buyer is in a relative state of certainty.

Other Unorthodox Times to Ask for a Referral

On the stall or nonsale—You have presented, but the deal isn't going to happen. At this point you have nothing to lose by asking for a referral. "Hey

John, I know this isn't the right time for you right now to go ahead and do this, but who do you know that would be interested in something like this?"

On the rejection—When the buyer rejects you with a flat-out no, again you have nothing to lose but to ask for a referral "John, I know this isn't for you, but who do you know that would be interested in something like this?"

On the opening—Open with a referral. "Hey, John, I know this probably isn't for you, but who do you know that would like to make 8–12 percent of their money secured by a first lien in real estate?" There is a saying in the money-raising sales industry: Come in for advice, come out with money. Come in for money, come out with advice.

8 Elements of Power and How To Increase Your Personal Power

"No man is wise enough or good enough to be trusted with unlimited power."
—Charles Colton

Power and the study of power has fascinated people for centuries. Power is seen and used in politics, in business, in love, in war, and seemingly in every human interaction there is some element of power being used. Power is simply defined as the ability to get things done, whether it be move an object across a room, influence an audience, or start or stop a war.

The value of power is so fundamental to human beings that it is indeed a fundamental value and need for every person. We must have a certain amount of power to be happy and get things done in life.

In negotiating, knowing how and when to use power is a way to create leverage and a stronger position. The eight elements of power that are shared in this book are for positioning purposes and can be stacked upon one another. You can use one type of power to gain advantage or use multiple elements of power at once for greater effect. The elements of power that we will explore in this section are:

Power of Legitimacy

Power of Prizes

Power of Punishment

Power of Integrity

Power of Charisma

Power of Expertise

Power of Timing

Power Of Information

Some readers may feel negative towards power as if power is about manipulating or harming people. When reading this section, understand that power is neutral; it is neither good nor bad and can be used for either good or evil.

Power is a tool and will be used as the wielders of power see fit. Consider the atomic bomb that was dropped on Japan at the end of World War II. Some would argue that the power of that bomb was horrible and killed and maimed many people along with destroying great Japanese cities at the time. The other side of the argument is that the power of the atomic bomb saved lives because it stopped a war that was dragging on too long and many more people would have died through prolonged fighting.

Regardless of your opinion on which side is right and which side is wrong, we can surely agree that such a bomb is powerful and can be used in a negative way to kill and destroy or in a positive way to prevent further wars.

Power of Legitimacy

The first element of power that must be learned is the power of legitimacy. As human beings we succumb to the "aura of legitimacy" portrayed by others in negotiations. If we see a person with the title of "vice president" we assume that he is important. If we see an official-looking price tag at the jewelry store, we believe that the price is real. Titles, the written word, and other trappings like business cards, brands, logos, and imagery all make up an "aura of legitimacy" that lend power to the person who appears to be legitimate.

Consider a medical doctor. When your medical doctor steps into his office and you have been waiting on the paper-covered examining table after the nurse took your blood pressure and checked your heart rate and weight, the legitimacy of someone who is called a doctor, wearing a white coat and looks the part creates an "aura of legitimacy" that makes us listen to whatever the doctor prescribes.

The doctor will write us an official prescription on an official piece of doctor paper, and we accept any drug he prescribes for us, because he is indeed a doctor. We do not consider the fact that the drug the doctor is prescribing for us is from a company he owns shares in, or the fact that the doctor may not actually know what is wrong with you. The fact is, the doctor is a doctor, he has a title, and appears legitimate, so we accept his word as true. That is the power of legitimacy.

The power of legitimacy extends to presidents or anyone else with power. The president of the United States would be expected to ride in a limo, not a Honda civic. He would be expected to have one of his staff carry his luggage up the steps into the White House and not carry it himself. If the president does not look and act like a president, he loses his power of legitimacy, and the people stop believing in him.

For you to have the power of legitimacy, you must use your title or create one if you do not have one yet. In my real estate office the entry level job for real estate is the "Vice President of Acquisitions." In reality, this job is entry level and anyone can be the "vice president," but when people in the industry get a call from the "vice president of acquisitions" they are more likely to talk to the legitimate-sounding person on the phone whether he has been in the business for five minutes or five years. Of course the vice president must have the confidence to carry out his "aura of legitimacy" for his power to be maintained.

Another way to create more power is to remove your first name from your business cards and all of your communications in general. Consider many successful authors H. G. Wells, J. K. Rowling, L. R. Hubbard, and anyone who uses their initials as their first name is forcing the other side to call them "Mr. Wells" or "Ms. Rowling." To remove your first name is to increase your power because it removes any chances of getting onto a first-name basis.

Another way to create power of legitimacy for yourself when negotiating is to use your office, automobile, or territory where you are surrounded by your own trappings of power. You may have your title on your desk, your awards you have won, your receptionist to make the other side wait in the lobby, the nice leather chair you sit in versus the plastic folding one that they sit in.

When you control the territory, you create legitimacy for yourself.

It is always more powerful to meet in your office surrounded by your trappings of power then to meet at your home or kitchen table. Real estate sales people understand the power of legitimacy and will typically lease a luxury car like a Mercedes, BMW, Porsche, Range Rover, or Lexus to create the aura of legitimacy when negotiating with clients. In reality, the salesperson may be broke and not have any money to make the payments, but it is always more powerful to negotiate in a beautiful, spotless, leather interior of a brand new Mercedes than it is to negotiate in a ten-year-old Toyota with kids' toys in the back, spilled milk on the seat, and a melted chocolate bar on the interior car mat.

Another way to create the power of legitimacy is to have a secretary screen and place your calls. You may find this pretentious, but the harder you are to access, the more perceived power you have.

In the insurance business, brand new agents who are male will get a female to record their voicemail message. In reality, these sales agents are dead broke and are just starting out in the industry; they cannot afford a secretary, but the female voice on the voicemail creates the "aura of legitimacy" that creates power and prestige for the new agent.

Other ways that people and companies use the power of legitimacy is through your positioning in the marketplace. You may be the:

1. Biggest
2. Smallest
3. Best
4. Worst
5. Oldest
6. Newest
7. Award winning, etc.

Being a positioned player in the marketplace adds to the legitimacy of your power.

When you have the power of legitimacy, what you will earn is respect. Consider the respect for the law that every day citizens have where you may be stuck at a red light in the middle of the night and no one is around. Rather than running the red light, most people will wait at the red light merely out of respect for the legitimate power of the law.

Tradition is another form of legitimate power. The power lies in the fact that "we have done this for a long time" and because "we have done this for a long time," we assume that the tradition is legitimate. We do not question old and outdated traditions merely on the fact that they have been around so long that they have become legitimate. With respect to legitimacy, consider the fact that in any endeavor you begin will start out illegitimate and brand new, but if you survive in the endeavor long enough, you eventually become legitimate.

Consider where the line of illegitimate to legitimate is? I challenge you to find it; you may find that the fact that you have "been around for a long time" suddenly makes you legit. You may know someone who has "been in the business for twenty years," who may say that to create legitimacy in their business practices, but consider the fact that they may have done the same year twenty times in a row and may not be any good at what they do. You may want someone who has been in the business for one year but with a stellar track record.

Along with tradition are established procedures or "company policies." Many businesses have price tags, and most consumers do not question the price tag on any item. Most items are negotiable when it comes to price, but the power of legitimacy and the written word make us comply with established procedures and prices.

Standard contracts and forms are another way to create the power of legitimacy. When a consumer makes a purchase, it always looks more legitimate to print a contract on three-ply carbon paper that creates a white copy, a yellow copy, and a pink copy with full return policies and procedures on it than it would be to write the customer's credit card number down on a cocktail napkin and stuff it in your pocket.

The standard contract with three copies allows the customer to take one home, the sales agent to keep one, and the company to process one copy. In reality, the contract is barely better than the napkin, but the power of legitimacy is what captures the heart and mind of the customer.

Power of Prizes

The term "breads and circuses" originated in Rome by the poet Juvenal in circa 100 A.D. The term identifies the problem in society where the populace only cares for the prizes of "breads" (free bread from the government and politicians in power) and "circuses" (gladiator and chariot games that entertain the masses). Since the average man only cares for breads and circuses, he no longer cares for his political birthright of political involvement and who is in power. The power of prizes has taken over a once powerful republic. Rome originated as a powerful stoic democracy where the people were involved in voting and controlling the government.

The government feared the power, not the other way around. When the elected politicians realized that they could buy the votes of the people with "prizes"—typically free grain, breads, and gladiator games, the political system became a race to the bottom to see who can give more prizes to the people in exchange for poorer and poorer governance. Throughout history, democracy only lasts for about 250 years until the people find out that they can vote themselves prizes and the system collapses.

"When the people find that they can vote themselves (prizes)
money, that will herald the end of the republic."
—Benjamin Franklin

Such is the power of the prize. When there is promise of a reward, people will give up their power in exchange for the prize or the reward. In Rome the people gave up their political involvement for free grain and free entertainment. Today in America, the same thing is happening; the people give up their involvement for breads and circuses, and this signals the end of the 250 year life span of democracy and the end of the republic, very much like Rome.

The ability to create a prize and reward the other side is a tremendous source of power. In a taxi cab company, the dispatcher has more power than the owner because he can reward the cab drivers with more jobs and in effect more money. The person who can give the prizes is the person with the power.

When you are negotiating in business, you can use the power of prizes when you position yourself. You are the best in the business and doing business with the best is a reward unto itself. There is always a market for the best and always a market for the cheapest. However, there is much more profit in being the best and positioned as the prize.

To create prize power in your business, you must put your personal reputation on the line to solve the buyer's problems. When you take on their problems, you are rewarding them; they are not rewarding you with the business. Most junior salespeople will feel like the customer is the prize and that the customer is rewarding the salesperson with the business. Professional salespeople who are the best in the business use the power of prizes to frame the situation differently. Professionals know that they are the prize and that they are rewarding the client with the best service in the industry—and that is why a great salesperson is a prize to be won by the customer.

When you utilize the power of prizes and frame yourself as the prize, you will have the confidence to ask your customer for all of their business rather than begging like a dog for a small share of the customer's table scraps. You are the prize to be won, so use prize power to your advantage.

Prize power can also be used as an intimidation factor. Whenever you feel as though the other side can reward you or give you a prize, you feel the power of prizes creep in. A junior salesperson may be intimidated with the prize power of his first $1,000 sale whereas a pro salesperson won't feel any pressure with a $100,000 sale. In fact, the more you ignore the power of prizes and ability that the other side has to reward you, the greater your power will be in relation to the other side.

Prize power can also be intimidating in the sexual arena. Consider a young man who is going on a date with a very beautiful woman who is "out of his league."

He may feel as though she is the prize and lose his confidence and his power when dealing with her. The same man can change his mind and tell himself that he is the prize and that she is lucky to be out with him and there will be an entire shift of power on the date.

Other prizes that may be available for intimidation purposes may be opportunities to do business in the future, access to a ski cabin, free trips, free food, opportunities for exposure, or any other rewards that you may find attractive. Maintain your power and do not be tempted by the power of prizes.

"A nation is born a stoic and dies an epicurean."

—Will Durant

---

sto·ic

ˈstōik/

noun

noun: **stoic**; plural noun: **stoics**; noun: **Stoic**; plural noun: **Stoics**

1.

2.   a person who can endure pain or hardship without showing their feelings or complaining.

Ep·i·cu·re·an

ˌepikyəˈrēən, ˌepiˈkyo͝orēən/

noun

noun: **Epicurean**; plural noun: **Epicureans**

1.

2.   a disciple or student of the Greek philosopher Epicurus.

a person devoted to sensual enjoyment, especially that derived from fine food and drink.

Power of Punishment

The power of punishment is the opposite of the power of prizes. Where the power of prizes alludes to the fact that the other side can reward you with intangible pleasurable benefits like money, fame, travel, love, sex, more business, or whatever else you desire, the power of punishment is the opposite of pleasure. The power of punishment is indeed the perception that the other side can punish or harm you rather than reward you.

Consider the intimidation factor of the power of punishment when a police officer pulls you over on the highway and has the power to give you a speeding ticket—or not. In that situation of intimidation, the police officer has the power of punishment.

Parents with children will use the power of prizes along with the power of punishment with their children. "if you finish your vegetables you will get an extra cookie with dessert . . . If you don't finish your vegetables, no playtime after dinner and you go straight to bed."

Power of Morality

The power of morality is awarded to those who have a consistent set of values and follow through on them. A person with high integrity and a set of unchanging values will always have more power than a person who changes his values frequently.

Consider the pope, the leader of the Catholic Church: although the Catholic Church has been responsible throughout history in killing, plunder, rape, murder, and theft and was responsible for one of the most terrible times in European history known as the Dark Ages, the pope, because of his unwavering values is one of the most powerful people on the planet.

How powerful is your decision-making ability? Are you a person who will stick to your decisions or go back on them? Do you take back an ex-lover or do you go crawling back when you are in a weak moment? The person who sticks to his decisions and his values will have the power of morality on his side.

The power of morality comes into play when you do what's right for the customer even if you send them to a competitor. Zappos, now a division of Amazon, is a major online shoe retailer where the sales staff is trained to find the right shoe for the customer even if they have to send the customer to a competitor.

This power of morality creates massive trust between the customer and Zappos. It wins loyal customers and huge sales in the long run. At Zappos they also use the power of morality when hiring staff. At the end of the two week paid staff training, they offer a $2,000 bonus to anyone who wants to quit on the spot and *not* work for the company.

This example of the power of morality gives the bad employees a chance to save face and leave before they cost the company money by offering bad customer service or working for a company that their heart is not invested in. When you bribe bad employees to leave, this builds massive trust on the entire Zappos team and creates a very strong culture of performance.

To maintain your power of morality, avoid setting standards and then breaking your own standards. Avoid saying that you never cut prices and then cut prices. This confuses the people around you and destroys your power.

The benefit of using the power of morality versus the power of prizes is that long-lasting values have a long term effect whereas the power of prizes and punishment have a short term effect. When you use the power of prizes to reward a child too often, very soon the child takes the prizes for granted and learns to expect rewards every time for the same behavior.

Building up your power of morality by having a strong set of values and sticking to them consistently brings trust and leverage into any negotiation. In fact, when negotiating against someone with strong values and high integrity, especially against cutting prices, you soon learn to not even ask for a concession. I have been an Apple Computers customer my entire life, and I used to ask for discounts on my new computer purchase every five years.

Apple will always respond with, "We don't discount our products," and in-fact, they do not give discounts to the public ever. Apple is so strong in the power of morality and sticking to their values that even after owning a Mac computer for years, you can still sell it for almost full value years later on the secondary market. The power of morality keeps Apple's brand strong because their products are excellent and thus a competitor's computer will sell for pennies on the dollar years later and the Mac computer will sell for nearly full price after years of use. Such is the power of morality and sticking to a consistent set of values.

Another trend where companies are using the power of morality to create massive trust is in the marketplace. Like Tom's Shoes or Roma Boots, who gives away a pair of new shoes or boots to a person in need for every pair that you buy.

These companies don't overplay this giving back in their marketing. Their goal isn't to completely destroy the local shoe makers and shoe economies; that is not part of moral power. Instead, they have a strong set of values, and this strong set of values helps Tom's Shoes and Roma Boots to become a major seller of shoes and boots worldwide regardless of the positive and negative effects of such morality.

Reverent power as an intimidation tool

As human beings we marvel at people who live by a consistent set of values. To be human is to be flawed, and at some point everyone may violate his or her values.

If you find that someone is using the power of morality against you, you may neutralize their power by 1) finding a precedent where the exception beat the rule or 2) establishing that the policy that they are enforcing on you may have worked in the past but is no longer relevant going forward. Rules were meant to be broken, and in negotiation, morals and ethics are merely weapons that one group of people will use against another group of people.

Power of Charisma

cha·ris·ma

kəˈrizmə/

noun

noun: **charisma**; plural noun: **charismata**

1. compelling attractiveness or charm that can inspire devotion in others.

"she enchanted guests with her charisma"

synonyms: charm, presence, personality, force of personality, strength of character; Moremagnetism, attractiveness, appeal, allure

"he lacks the charisma we look for in our salespeople"

2. a divinely conferred power or talent.

The power of charisma is hard to classify and hard to identify. Charisma is a "gift from god" or a "special talent" such as the ability to heal or prophesize. In modern terms, charisma is the ability to capture the heart and mind of another person and gain support or devotion.

Another way to look at the power of charisma would be the power of personality, power of celebrity, or the power of being liked. We always wish to please people that we like and the power of charisma can be completely magical. Consider the special treatment that rock stars get when they travel across the country. Celebrities get free cars, free travel, free food, and a multitude of other benefits from their power of charisma.

To be likable and charismatic is to be powerful. People have a hard time saying no to a person they like. Consider a cute little three-year-old girl asking for a cookie. She is cute and has charisma; and you will give her the cookie.

Charismatic power as an intimidation factor

The power of charisma can be very intimidating in that we are less inclined to ask for concessions from people that we like. In fact, a charismatic negotiator can often make deals that would be impossible for an uncharismatic person to make. If you study top salespeople or negotiators, you will find the power of charisma as an intangible X factor they have either developed or were born with.

Power of Expertise

When you project more expertise on a subject than other people, you have power over them. Your doctor, auto mechanic, plumber, and even your maid will have expertise you don't. A waiter at a fancy restaurant will have the power of expertise when making recommendations to you. We all want to be guided by experts and as human beings we are trained socially to look to experts to learn what we should think about any particular subject.

Expertise as an Intimidation Factor

Do not be intimidated by someone who appears to be an expert. The expert is merely someone who is at least one step ahead of the person they are advising. Oftentimes, experts are merely people who are self-proclaimed experts and may not even have any special knowledge or expertise at all. Consider a realtor who claims to be the local area expert. What qualifies him to be the expert? The fact that he lives on a street in the neighborhood? He is merely the expert because he calls himself the expert.

Conversely, when someone questions your expertise on a matter and you may lack the expertise to maintain power, simply say "That is not my area of expertise, but my team is the finest in the business, and I have someone with that expertise on my team."

Using different and specific language is a major ploy for using the power of expertise to gain advantage over others. Doctors and lawyers will use different language with you to appear more technical and more powerful, so get them to speak in plain English to take the expertise and intimidation factor away. You can strip the power of expertise completely away from people using special language on you to get them to explain the technical jargon-using fourth-grade language or, as I like to say, explain that to a three-year-old when the three-year-old is me!

Power of Timing

The power of timing is found when people who normally don't have any power suddenly have power over you. Consider the clerk at the government office who has no power to choose how he does his job when suddenly you show up his desk and need something from him. This government worker with limited power typically will exercise power over you because in this situation and this specific timing, he will have all the power and you have none. Generally, people with very little power love to use it when they get a chance.

You can see the power of timing with building inspectors, desk clerks, secretaries, government workers etc. These people have very little power in real life, but under certain timings and circumstances, their power is magnified immensely.

Power of Information

With the proliferation of computers in the 1990s, the Industrial Age ended when the Berlin Wall came down and we entered the Information Age. The power of information is extremely valuable when negotiating because the sharing of information bonds people together. When you share information with your customers, you create value, and this shared information bonds the customer to you. Pharmaceutical reps typically can only book meetings with busy doctors if they have new information about a drug or specific research. I used to work for a company in Canada that shared more free information in the marketplace than any other competitor, and in a few short years the startup company grew to have multimillion-dollar revenue and became the fortieth fastest growing company in the country. Such is the power of information and its ability to build trust in a negotiation.

Information Power as an Intimidation Factor

Secrets and withheld information can be used to manipulate the confidence levels of negotiators in any negotiation. Secrets and withheld information may increase or decrease your confidence in any situation.

Stacking Power

If you study top salespeople and top negotiators around the world, you will notice that they will use multiple types of power at once and will "stack" power for maximum leverage and advantage. A sales leader in most industries will use all eight types of power to his advantage, namely:

Power of Legitimacy—A sales leader will have a fancy title "regional vice president," he will look like a president and act like the owner of the company.

Power of Prizes—The sales leader will have some specific reward or prize for taking action today, perhaps a special discount or rebate for taking action now.

Power of Punishment—The sales leader will also have something that will be lost for those who do not take action today.

Power of Morality—The sales leader will appeal to the power of morality by serving a higher purpose or sticking to a strong set of values of doing what is right for the customer. He may even donate a percentage of his profits to charity to show morality.

Power of Charisma—The sales leader will be charismatic and well liked to many types of people. He will typically be physically fit, well dressed, well spoken, well-mannered and have a good sense of humor with a high degree of agreeableness.

Power of Expertise—The sales leader will be framed as an expert in his field.

Power of Timing—The sales leader will have the power of timing on his side in that now is the perfect time to act on his offer.

Power of Information—The sales leader will use information to his advantage and may offer you a free report, free book, or any other materials you will need to make a decision today.

Other Forms of Power

Power of Crazy

To convince the other side that you are crazy is to have power over them. You are unpredictable and you are powerful. The power of unpredictability is terrifying to most intelligent, rational people. We like to be able to predict the outcomes of dealing with another person and nothing is more powerful than a man with nothing to lose or everything to gain.

Power of Risk Displacement, Risk Sharing, or Risk Reversal

One way to create power in a negotiation is to give a risk reversal guarantee where the seller will offer a money-back guarantee if their product does not perform. To manipulate risk, displace it, share it, or reverse it, which is extremely powerful at the bargaining table. Besides reversing risk, you can also share the risk of the upside or downside of a deal. Consider a real estate syndicate where instead of contributing $1,000,000 to a large real estate project, investors are much more comfortable to break the $1,000,000 into one hundred $10,000 units. A smaller risk with a smaller reward can be very powerful in this situation.

Power of Confusion

As an extension of the power of information is the power of confusion. They say in sales that a confused mind does not buy. However, creating confusion by having too many moving parts or too much complexity can create power for you as a seller or a buyer. Creating confusion can create need, and need disempowers the other side and makes them more willing to buy your solution. Use confusion to your advantage by offering a confusing problem and your simple solution.

Power of Competition

The person who has more options always has more power in any negotiation. Consider the power of competition, when there are multiple buyers—say ten, fifteen, or twenty buyers for a single property. The property will enter into a bidding war where the buyers will strip their offers of conditions and escalate their buying price to irrational levels just to win. The human spirit is very competitive and although we may not admit to loving a competition, we all love to win. Whenever you can get multiple people competing for one job or one opportunity, you will create leverage and advantage just by using the power of competition.

The Stall—Multi-Call Selling, Setting the Next Appointment

Some buyers you will be able to close on the first engagement and you should always aim to close in the shortest path possible. However, you will never be able to close every buyer on the first engagement. Your goal as a salesperson, however is to get a simple "Yes or no" decision as to whether this product is for them. Is this worth pursuing more?

At the end of the sales presentation there are five outcomes:

1. Yes
2. Yes, with condition
3. Maybe
4. No with condition
5. No

You have done your job as a salesperson when you are eliminating all maybes from your life. It's either a yes, yes with a condition, no, or no with a condition.

When you begin to set a meeting, whether they are phone meeting or in person meeting, you want to be in control as much as possible. You want to stay in rapport which is:

1. Sharp as a tack
2. Enthusiastic as hell
3. An expert in your field.

Protecting your time and avoiding phone tag are parts of being an expert and a professional. The more professional you act yourself, the more professional your prospects will treat you.

As a rule, I never accept "I'll call you back" or "call me back next week," which will put you into an endless game of voicemails, phone tag and wasted time. Instead, say "Okay, John, I understand there are some things you have to do before we can get started. Let's set a phone meeting, exactly one week today, same day, same time. I'll call you at this number. I've got you in my calendar; am I in yours?"

The easiest path to a yes is one-week, same day, same time, which is likely open in the buyer's schedule.

If the buyer doesn't show up to the second phone meeting leave him a message "John, this is [[YOURNAME]] from [[XYZ COMPANY]]. We had a meeting tonight scheduled at 7 PM, so reach me back at 555–555–5555. I hope everything is okay."

Also send a text and an email, then wait fifteen minutes. If the buyer doesn't show up to the phone meeting, this is meaningless: life gets in the way, he had other priorities; it does not mean he does not want your offer. Keep contacting him in a professional manner with a second voicemail, text, and email.

After two voicemails, texts, and emails, you can do one final voicemail that will usually make him surface: "Hey John, it's [[FIRST NAME]] calling from [[XYZ COMPANY]] and I haven't heard back from you. Hope everything is okay. I'm leaving you a third voicemail to let you know I will not be chasing you, and if I do not hear from you, I'm going to assume you are not interested in the program we spoke about earlier. If you still are interested, you can call me back at 555–555–5555 on my direct line; otherwise good luck to you."

Also send that text and email. You will typically notice that he will call you back because of the "I'm not going to call or chase you anymore" message. If he doesn't reply he is either:

1. Out of the country and is not accessing his messages or
2. You aren't a priority.

If you aren't a priority, rotate him to a lower position in your lead stack and re-prospect him later.

You also want to be clear when doing phone meetings or in person meetings about your process and "If you like it, this is what's going to happen." I typically operate on a one or two meeting sale with a limit of three. Let the prospect know that they should be able to decide in a certain amount of time to avoid time wasters.

On a three-meeting system, 30 percent of my business is closed on the first meeting, 40 percent on the second and 30 percent on the third. There is value in going to three meetings in rare circumstances with clear limits to the prospect about how decisions are to be made. When I began my sales career in private equity, the company I worked for *never* closed on the first meeting as they believed it could not be done. Some salespeople had an undefined number of meetings and called it "relationship selling," which I believed to be nonsense. I shortened the sales cycle to close on the first meeting and it worked—people bought. Most sales were done in one or two meetings with a rare third, which saved me huge amounts of time and also put me into the top ranks of salespeople almost immediately.

PART FOUR

TURNING PRO—BECOMING A TOP 1
PERCENT SALESPERSON—MACRO GAME

PART FOUR

IV

When I was seventeen, I had a burning desire to sell, it was in my blood! Every summer in high school I "had to get a job" to get money for the next year and later in university it was to pay next year's tuition. The jobs that always attracted me were the sales jobs—vacuums, insurance, financial services, real estate, private equity, energy contracts, and I would always get started with a company and then my family who had a horribly negative belief about selling would resist me so much, I would quit.

I would hear things like "they aren't going to pay you!," "Sales organizations are crooks!," "You won't find any leads!," "Who is going to buy from you, you're just a kid!?," "How are you going to win business?," and "Where are your customers going to come from?." Negative nonsense poisoned my emotional mind until I got a safe secure job painting houses in the summer and the same people said, "Good honest work.," "Safe secure pay.,"

"Guaranteed money.," and suggested I go work for the government (as most of my family does).

The negativity came from the fact that my father had taken a short career in sales and was fired right about the time my younger brother was born. Back then, they paid large base salaries, expense accounts, car accounts all sorts of luxurious things many salespeople don't get from their companies these days. I assume he survived off his base pay, and the "up and down money" irritated my mother who was a government teacher and got paid every two weeks.

The real problem was that my father was an amateur salesperson, which is common in the sales industry. Sales is an industry filled with amateurs, training amateurs, attracting amateurs, and nearly all of the bad things said about sales and selling come from an amateur's reputation.

I recently had my father join me at one of my negotiation classes in which we have each student do thirty live negotiations against real opponents for real money. The class is set up like a tournament, and the winner ends up with the most real money, and the weaker negotiators lose money as the weekend goes on. Out of forty-six negotiators, my father placed 44th, and #45 and #46 left early and didn't finish he tournament.

My father was indeed an amateur who never read a book, took a class, or hired a coach or mentor to make him better. When I was driving him home after the event he said, "If I knew this information twenty years ago, I'd be a multimillionaire today! I let so many deals and opportunities slip by . . ." I kept my hands on the wheel and said, "Yup, all it takes is a $20 book and a few thousand dollars to go to a class."

In sales there are three levels of professional:

1. Amateurs
2. Pros
3. Super-pros

Amateurs are amateurs because they take the two-week training class at the beginning of their sales career and stop there; they don't bother to read books on selling, negotiation, or marketing etc. to become better. They don't take a class or hire a performance coach or mentor to bring them to the next level. In the world of cause and effect: amateur input, amateur output. Most amateurs in sales do not make much money at all.

In the world of real estate, most real estate salespeople live below the poverty line because they are amateur salespeople who do not study or take the profession seriously.

Pros are lifelong learners who understand that becoming a professional salesperson is technical and takes as much study as becoming a medical doctor, lawyer, business executive, or any other white collar professional. If you want to make professional income that is the top 1 percent of your industry, you must put in professional input—that means training harder than anyone else, reading more, being in better shape, having better professional hygiene, stronger ethics, a better personal brand, a better image, and overall better skills and professional work ethic. Sales is the highest paid job in the world for someone who trains like a pro, plays like a pro, and gets results like a pro.

The only thing that separates amateurs from pros is that to turn pro, a person must decide he wants to be the top 1 percent. I believe that if you are in selling you should aim to be no less than the top 4 percent of income earners in your country. At the time of writing right now, that's around $120,000 in Canada where I live. The top 1 percent income earners earn $250,000. You must aim to be first in the top 10 percent, then the top 5 percent, 4 percent, then 1 percent.

Super-pros are the superstars of the industry. These people are game changers earning extraordinary incomes. They run wildly successful selling practices and often train amateurs to be pros. Super pros are the top

0.5 percent or 0.1 percent of their game and many are earning in excess of $1,000,000 a year. Many super-pros build brands around themselves and turn into business moguls.

Why You Need to Be a Pro or Super-Pro in Today's World

In today's world, the market is getting too competitive. Technology is gobbling up jobs at a faster pace than ever and there is less and less room for the amateurs at the bottom. As they say, "It's crowded at the bottom, but it's lonely at the top." If you are making the decision to be in sales, it is your absolute utmost ethical duty to reach your potential and at the very least get to pro status. Personal taxes are higher than ever, expenses keep creeping up, and inflation keeps getting higher and higher eating away at your earnings. $250,000 isn't a lot of money anymore. Where I live in Winnipeg, Manitoba, Canada you can buy a 100 year-old-crack house for $100,000 when the median home is currently $320,000 annually!

The average household income in Winnipeg is only $70,000, which works out to only $35,000 per working person! In a recent article when asking the wealthy how much money they needed to be wealthy, they replied "$100,000,000." A millionaire is the new middle class along with doctors, lawyers and dentists who used to be upper middle class.

The world is changing, and you must be at least a pro to make the profession of selling a worthwhile endeavor.

Power Prospecting

"The leads are weak!" says one of the salesmen in the famous movie *Glengarry Glenn Ross* in which Alec Baldwin replies "You're weak!"

So your company didn't give you any leads? Big deal. Leads costs companies massive amounts of money, and I know because I frequently buy them for my own sales team and feed them daily. Leads on a silver platter come at premium. You might think leads handed to you are a real bonus, but in reality, whenever the company hands you a lead, they need to water down your commission somewhere in the equation to give you less money per sale.

The more you can hunt and kill your own leads, the higher your commissions will be. In one of my companies, the sales team earns 25 percent if I feed them the lead, 35 percent if they bring in the lead and close it, amazingly, in two years of operation, the salespeople have always resorted to the path of least resistance and have focused exclusively on the 25 percent leads that are handed to them rather than picking up the phone and bringing in their own leads—amazing!

It is human nature to always look for ways to conserve energy, and that means time, effort, energy, and money. Salespeople are no different; if you give them an easier way, they will always degrade themselves to the easiest, lowest paid activity possible to conserve energy, it's a fact! This is why salespeople erroneously start changing presentations and cutting corners to make it easier for them, but it also is the first thing that causes their sales to slip and decline and eventually death spiral into a "dry spell" of zero sales.

5 Proven and Profitable Sources of Leads

The Power Base—The first place you always want to look for leads is in your power base. To create power base, simply get out a piece of paper and write down every single person you know—you can get out your phone address book, your email list, and your social media accounts and compile everyone into one massive list.

No matter how unconnected you are, every person should have at least 150 people they know and can remember. Your power base is where your best and biggest opportunities will come from because they know you, like you, and trust you. Some people object to the power base, saying, "I don't want to sell or talk to my friends and family." As a rebuttal, most people who say that are broke or have a poverty mentality.

Once you have your list, you can organize it into first circle, second circle, third circle by the following criteria:

1. First circle knows you, knows what you do, and would 80 percent buy from you

2. Second circle kind of knows you and has a 20 percent chance to buy from you

3. Third circle does not know you and has a less than 10 percent chance of buying from you

Your job is to work your power base and bring as many people into your first circle as possible. You can start off with the first circle, call them, catch up on your relationship, explain to them what you are doing and if they know of anyone who would be interested in that kind of thing. This is where a ton of business lies because these people have an 80 percent chance of buying from you when the time is right. The first circle can also be a great source of referrals.

Once first circle calls are done, then you call your second circle, which you know less well than you first circle, have a similar conversation and invite them to have lunch with you. Once you have broken bread with these people, they are now in your first circle.

The third circle you do not know that well, so you will send them a post-card that reads, "Hey, we haven't spoken in a while, was thinking of you, let's do lunch!" and let them call you to bring them into the second and finally the first circle.

As a professional salesperson you should never eat lunch alone; instead, eat lunch with someone who can buy from you—a potential customer or a potential referral source—because your network is your net worth. Always work your powerbase and go back to it for the best source of leads. Too many salespeople give up on their powerbases or forget about them, it's your main source of power. Do anything you can: join country clubs, tennis clubs, golf clubs, or the best gym or spa in town to increase the quality and quantity of your powerbase.

Existing Customers—The second best source of leads for you as a salesperson is your company's existing lead database or book of business. These customers have already walked over the line of money and made a purchase. They already like the company enough to buy, they like the product and the brand enough to buy and repeat customers are seven times easier to sell than cold traffic. In fact, there is virtually no company on the face of the earth that can transmute cold traffic into gold in a reliable way.

Cold traffic is where most marketers, salespeople, branding people, and everyone turn to for new revenue, but it's also the animal that can never be tamed! Cold traffic it is always changing, and whatever works today in marketing likely won't work tomorrow. Cracking cold traffic is the holy grail that every company wants but almost none can do efficiently. Therefore, focusing on those who have already bought will result in the quickest path to money for you. When I took over the Winnipeg office for a private equity company I was working for, not a single salesperson was calling the existing database.

There were tens of thousands of leads who had attended seminars, seen the product, liked it enough and no one ever followed up. Instead, what the salespeople in eleven offices across the country would do is wait for the touring seminar to come through town, get a huge pile of hot juicy fresh leads, call them, work them, then do nothing. They called it "relationship selling." What a pile of nonsense. I sat down in the Winnipeg office, opened up the database and began calling the people who had been left behind. My script was simple:

"Hey [[THEIR NAME]], is this [[THEIR NAME]]?

Hey [[THEIR NAME]], it's [[YOUR NAME]], [[YOUR POSITION]], calling from [[YOUR COMPANY]] on behalf of the founder [[FOUNDER NAME]]. I've just taken over the Winnipeg office, and I noticed that you attended one of our events in the past and no one has called you in a while; got a minute?

"The reason for the call is just a quick customer service call to see how things were going with your real estate investments and to reopen the lines of communication . . ."

Most customers love to hear a quick customer service call from a company they bought from, know, like, and trust. It's your chance to give them information on the new developments, new deals, new products, and new offers and check in on how their account is doing etc. and also a fantastic source of business and referrals for you. Customers who feel valued will share your name with others!

Paying for marketing for new customers—This is the favorite for salespeople and the least favorite for the company. Lazy, loser, amateur salespeople will sit around and wait for the next advertising barrage to hit and take the walk-in traffic, the inbound calls, and the easy low hanging fruit because it expends the least energy, but you have two major problems with new customers:

1. **They cost a fortune to acquire through the marketing department.** Depending on where you are in the marketing campaign's lifecycle, the leads may be at the cheapest they can be bought or the end of the cycle where the costs go up geometrically per customer. You can't rely on the company's big pockets to reach in and feed you every time you

are hungry. These leads are a bonus, a gift from God, the holy grail for salespeople. If you are given leads by your company that are hot and fresh and new—hallelujah! You found a great place to work. However, you don't know how reliably these people are going to come into your funnel and how often because marketing always presents its own challenges, and you could wake up one day to find that the campaign is burned out and there are no more leads until the marketing department "figures it out" again. Do not rely on these leads for your success.

2. **They don't know you, may not like you, and certainly don't trust you**—These people are cold; they are the general public; they don't trust anyone because they have been screwed and burned so many times by unscrupulous amateur salespeople. As Zig Ziglar says, "If a cat jumps up on a hot stove and burns his paw, he won't stay away from stoves, he'll stay out of the kitchen!" Buyers today have many reasons to distrust anything marketing or a salesperson tells them because there has been copious amounts of unethical advertising over the years and ultimately lying, cheating, and stealing to make a few dollars by too many players. Cold traffic is terrified of you because you might sell them something, they might do something stupid, they might lose money on your offer, and there is a myriad of trust building exercises that must be done to build trust with these leads before they can turn into customers.

Smart Outbound cold calling: There is value in outbound cold calling, in real estate acquisitions, I have my salespeople call fifty realtors a day, cold. Why? Because relationships are built through communication, and these people have the potential to enter the powerbase overtime as a source of leads. You might pick up the newspaper (yes, they still exist) and call companies with ads advertised if you are selling ads, or contractor advertisements if you sell things to contractors, but this is highly niche and applies to each sales profession and industry separately.

Bill Bartmann, the billionaire, used to say, "If you want to catch a fish, most people would go to the ocean, a river, a lake, or a stream, I say go to a fish farm.

Sure, you pay a fee to get in, but when you walk by the tank, the fish hear your boots and know it's feeding time, so they come to the top, ready for food and you scoop up as many as you want. "If you are going to look for a fish, find the "fish farm" for your niche, and pay something to get inside, because it's usually worth it.

Blind Outbound Cold Calling/knocking doors: If you have a good enough script for this or if your product or service permits, knocking doors and blind cold calling can work. I still prefer all methods above to this brute force, inefficient grind-until-you-die method, but some people make entire careers out of it and it still works.

I have never sold cars, but I heard of a famous car salesman who would call people out of the phone book and say "Hey, is this John? Hey John, it's Mike Jones calling from Main Street Cadillac. We have a brand-new car being delivered to your house this afternoon and I wanted to confirm the address was 123 Fakestreet.

The buyer on the other end would go, "What?! I didn't order a brand new Cadillac?!," the salesman would have their address and name from the phone book and then would enter a conversation with them explaining that some wires must have been crossed, but while they were on the phone, were they in the market for a new car?

This particular gentlemen made a career off of this. If you have the script and it's efficient for you, do it until it doesn't work anymore! Personally, I prefer the power base, existing customers and marketing customers to this, which should be more than enough to fill up your sales day productively every day.

Time Management—The Ideal Sales Day

They say that the real rock stars are either waking up at 5:00 AM or going to bed at 5:00 AM—either way, 5:00 AM is part of the equation. Typically, salespeople have to operate during the day so I will make a schedule around starting at 5:00 AM rather than going to bed at 5:00 AM. If you are an artist, creative, visionary, writer, or a night salesperson, you might go to bed at 5:00 AM, but that is taxing on the body overtime as the cortisol and hormones don't balance right. Your body was meant to get up with the sun; its rhythms work with the circadian cycle of sunlight and darkness.

The modern world with artificial light has really changed people's schedules to very odd hours, and people are doing things that were never possible in history before, like eating a large pizza at 1:00 AM on the couch in front of the TV. One hundred years ago, or further back in history, that was impossible; there was no delivery of pizza at 1:00 AM, there was no blue light shining in your eyes, or TVs to be watched. One hundred years ago, when it got dark, you went to bed; candles and electric light weren't very good.

The Ideal Sales Day

5:00 AM: Wake up, start heading to the gym, stick an audiobook in your ears, start mind feeding. The more you feed your mind, the better you will be. If you fail to plant flowers in your mind, weeds will grow. The absence of positive messages always defaults to negative messages, so stick something positive in your ears the second you wake up; it will motivate you to keep going and get out of bed. If you listen to an audiobook first thing in the morning throughout your entire morning routine, in the car and in between meetings, you can consume a book a week, making fifty-two books a year. The average CEO reads sixty books a year. If you read fifty books a year for four years you are likely as smart as someone with a graduate degree in university. Do it for ten years and that's 500 books—you will be an international scholar.

First thing out of bed and last thing at night is also your most creative time. Often you can solve problems you can't solve in the middle of the day at 5:00 am when everything is quiet. Why? No distractions. Some people like to write out their goals first thing in the morning; as long as you do it sometime before you get to work and review your vision plan for your life, you will be on track.

6:00–7:00 AM Get up. Go the gym walk, jog or run at least two miles a day as recommended by sales trainer Brian Tracy. Do your workout with your audiobook in your ears still, then have a steam or sauna, shower, and shave.

7:00–8:00 AM Get dressed/Breakfast/get to work with the audiobook is still playing in your ears. You now have three hours of reading done while also preparing for the day. An ideal diet is low in fat, low in carbs, and no artificial sugar. Most very high performing people do not eat meat or drink alcohol.

8:00–9:00 AM Strategic planning—This is your hour to really review your strategic plan for the day: how are you going to get the most out your day today? Review your vision plan, your journal, or whatever resources you use to plan your life.

I personally keep a one-year vision plan with every detail written out in advance about my life, both personal and business. I offer this plan to others as a program called "Your Best Self," which you can purchase from my company online.

I also keep two journals: one is my high-performance journal with my ninety-day goals broken down into step by step actions, and the other is the black book which is a book I use to track my sales meetings and negotiations daily. Both the high-performance journal and the black book can be purchased online from my company.

9:00–10:00 AM Set up your people for the day—current business—If you have an executive assistant or a team, set them up for the day and give them goals to hit; otherwise, focus on the current business you have in the pipeline.

10:00–11:00 AM emails and callbacks—current business—Only do emails once and at a maximum twice per day. Generally business does not happen over email; it mostly happens over the phone or in person, so I typically avoid email at all costs as it's usually people looking to take your time. Limit this use. Check your voicemails, make your callbacks from the day before, and focus on current business in the pipeline.

11:00 AM-12:00 noon—Current business—Focus on current business in the pipeline.

12:00 noon-1:00 PM Lunch—If you are going to eat lunch, go out with a customer; otherwise pack an extremely light lunch and eat it while working. Don't go out for lunch with your sales buddies and waste time together. Only eat lunch with people who have the potential of being a customer or bringing you customers, or keep working and eat light.

15-minute nap. This is key to eighteen hours of being awake each day. A fifteen-minute powernap, one where you slip out of consciousness for a few moments and then reenter will refresh your mind and bring creative solutions to the top of your mind. Why? Because when you are entering or exiting consciousness is when the creative mind is coming to the surface. I like to break my day up with two fifteen-minute naps if possible so I am never going for more than six hours without breaking consciousness. Some people like Ray Dalio (successful hedge fund manager with a net worth of $17 billion) practice mediations; a fifteen-minute nap is a primitive form of meditation.

1:15–6:00 PM New business and potential sales meetings—This is your zone to earn and win new business. If you make sales through sales meetings, only schedule them in the afternoon if you can; it will keep you more organized.

6:30 PM Debrief for day, fifteen-minute nap—Reconcile what you did for the day and write down what needs to be done for tomorrow in your journals to avoid loose ends.

7:00–9:00 PM If you have a family you may want to spend time with them. Your kids only need to see you one or two hours a day if you are a father and if you are a mother, they need to see you more. But it's a myth that you need to be around all the time for your kids; your kids have their own lives and don't want to see you as much as you think. If you don't have a family, you will likely be doing meetings in this time or prospecting more if your industry allows it.

9:00–10:00 PM The key to going to bed on time is to actually get in the bed. Get in bed, mind feed with a real paperback book, and review your goals before going to sleep. If you review your goals before going to sleep, your mind will have a chance to work on them while sleeping and you will wake up with new solutions that have "magically" appeared. The only magic is the power of the subconscious mind and what Napoleon Hill calls infinite intelligence in *Think and Grow Rich*.

11:00 PM-5:00 AM Sleep. You only need six hours of sleep to sustainably maintain your life. In my experience four hours eventually breaks you down, and eight is too much, but six can sustainably be done over time. As Arnold Schwarzenegger says, "Everyone has twenty-four hours in a day.

You have to sleep six, so that leaves you with eighteen hours to yourself"
How you manage those hours is up to you and directly affects your income.

But what if my sales day looks different?

Some people might like at this schedule and say, "That's too long of a
day," "That's too much planning," "That's not going to work for me in my
industry," or "I'm different, my industry is different." I would beg to differ.
When people say, "I'm different," or "My industry is different," it usually is
an excuse to let them off the hook from doing all the things they think they
should have been doing all along. People are fundamentally the same, and
industries are fundamentally the same.

If your hours are different, so be it. This schedule was learned from a
$100,000,000 man and helped me make over $1,000,000 a year and reach
the top fraction of 1 percent in my industry, so if you are okay with staying
where you are in life, stick to your schedule, but if you want to level up,
adopt the 5:00 AM schedule.

Keys to Ongoing Success (Metrics)

"Actions equal dollars, dollars don't equal actions."
—*Gerry Mason, Sales Trainer*

Sales is a contact sport, which means you must make contacts to win.
Whenever a salesperson is underperforming, it usually equates to not
enough sales activity being generated, also known as calls being made or
secondly, it's the execution of a well-thought-out scripted presentation and
close.

Years ago, while working in the private equity industry, I was trained by
a gentlemen who had been selling vacuums and other direct products his
whole life but was trained in school as an engineer. He had the mind of
process, a mathematical way to achieve a desired result. I liked the idea of

mathematically being able to determine my earnings based on my actions because most of the negative things I heard my family say about selling was "Selling is luck," "Sometimes there's money, sometimes there isn't," or "It's up and down." If your business or sales career is "up and down" be assured, you are operating as an amateur. A professional knows with a degree of certainty that the law of certainty works.

The law of certainty: certain things performed in a
certain way will yield certain results, certainly!

Professional salespeople have a system to keep their pipeline full and money coming in every day. I will repeat that. As a business, you the salesperson need to be bringing in money every day. If you are a business you must sell every day, and as a salesperson you need to sell every day. When selling private equity, I would not go home until I made enough sales to cover my daily expenses because I knew that actions equal dollars.

The question you might want to ask yourself is, what does it cost you to go to work every day? Most people have $30,000 of expenses starting out in life which is $2,500 a month, which is $125 dollars a day for twenty working days of the month. That's what most people need to break even and live an extremely modest life. If you are a salesperson with $30,000 of expenses and you only manage to make $125 a day in commissions at the end of the year, you made $30,000 in earnings minus $30,000 commission so you made $0 for the year! It's not worth it.

You need to know your numbers going in so that you can multiply your expenses by ten with earnings and stay ahead of the curve. As a salesperson, as a business of one, you need to be profitable. If you don't want to be profitable, you can always work at McDonalds or for the government. I heard they are both hiring.

Personal Business Plan—The Fishbowl

Calls lead to conversations. Those conversations lead to meetings. Booked leads in meetings can lead to closes and lead to dollars collected for your personal business.

I don't know what industry you are in, but I'll use a fifty-call day as an example and a benchmark to illustrate the path to money.

Definitions

Calls = # of times the phone was dialed

Conversations = # of times you spoke to the decision maker

Meetings = Meetings with the intent of purchasing the product or service

Close = What it's worth for you to close a deal and earn in commissions

Daily

50 Calls a day

10 Conversations

2 Meetings booked

Weekly

250 calls a week

50 Conversations

10 meetings booked

Meetings

10 Meetings booked

3 Close

Each close is worth $1,800

3 x $1,800 = $5,400 for the week

Monthly

1,000 calls a month

200 conversations

40 meetings conducted

12 meetings closed

12 closes at $1,800 a close = $21,600 for the month

Annually

50-week year assuming 2 weeks off

250 calls x 50 weeks = 12,500 calls

2,500 conversations at a 20 percent pick up the phone rate

500 meetings at a 20 percent book meetings

150 closes at a 30 percent close rate

150 closes at $1,800 a close = $270,000 annual earnings

> *In this scenario you made $21.60 every time you dialed the phone whether the customer picked up the phone or not!*

What we have illustrated here is a very simple business plan for a single salesperson and how he is going to run his year. It all starts with a certain number of calls per day because without the top line, there can be no bottom line. As Steve Jobs, the founder of Apple used to say, "Take care of the top line and everything else will sort itself out."

You want to be motivated by dollars per dial because you don't control anything else. The only number you control on the entire plan is your dials, and everything else requires someone else to respond. That is why you must measure yourself in dollars per dial so that you know your optimum amount of activity. In private equity, I knew that roughly $8 a call was where I needed to be. If I was making $1,000 a call, I wasn't making enough calls and if I was making $1 a call, my script or process was broken.

Track your numbers in a personal spreadsheet grid called "the fishbowl."

I don't know what industry you are in, but I'll use a fifty-call day as an example and a benchmark to illustrate the path to money:

	A	B	C	D	E	F	G	H	I	J
1	Week Of	Monday, January 15th	WEEK		1				Fishbowl V: Version 1.0	
2									Setter Script ABCvAndrew1.0	
3									Closer Script: T3CloserScript1.0	
4	Setter Name:	John Grinder								
5										
6			Monday	Tuesday	Wednesday	Thursady	Friday	Saturday	Sunday	TOTALS/averages
7		Calls	50	64	50	52	51	25	0	292
8		Conversations	15	13	20	8	14	6	0	76
9		Closes	2	2	3	1	0	1	0	9
10		Apps	2	2	3	1	0	2	0	10
11		App Grades	AB	AB	ABC	A	nil	BB	0	
12		Revenue $ Collected	$600.00	$600.00	$700.00	$20.00	$0.00	$150.00	$0.00	2070
13		Commission $ Collected	$300.00	$300.00	$350.00	$10.00	$0.00	$75.00	$0.00	1035
14		Backend Comision Earned	$1,800.00	$0.00	$0.00	$0.00	$0.00		$0.00	1800
15		$/Dial	$42.00	$4.69	$7.00	$0.19	$0.00	$3.00	#DIV/0!	$9.71
16										
17	Closer Name	Michael Gritty								TOTALS/AVERAGES
18		1st Meetings Conducted	2	0	2	0	0	1	0	5
19		Meetings Rescheduled	1	0	0	0	0	0	0	1
20		Meeting No Shows	1	0	0	0	0	0	0	1
21		2nd Meeting Conducted	0	0	0	0	0	0	0	0
22		3rd Meeting Conducted	0	0	0	0	0	0	0	0
23		Closes	1	0	0	0	0	0	0	1
24		Sales Booked	$ 18,000.00	$ -	$ 18,000.00	$ -	$ -	$ 60,000.00	$ -	$ 96,000.00
25		$ Dollars Collected	$ 18,000.00	$ -	$ 18,000.00	$ -	$ -	$ 60,000.00	$ -	$ 96,000.00
26		$ In Payment Plan	0	0	0	0	0	0	0	0
27										
28		CLOSER MEETINGS							Closing %	20.00%
29		Prospect Names	Meeting 1	Meeting 2	Meeting 1	Notes				

To download your own fishbowl file go to 7LevelSelling.com/fishbowl

How to Fix the Machine if It's Broken

The small business plan you have made is a machine. If you put the top number into the machine, the bottom number will spit out money. The problem is, sometimes the machine breaks down. You must track your personal numbers every day so that you know what your dollar per call is and can stay at optimum levels of performance. Use the "Fishbowl" to keep track of your activity. Your sales manager should also have a team fishbowl to figure out where the team sales are at and who needs additional training.

Some problems to fix:

Calls but no pickups = Wrong time of day to be calling, or dead leads, or the area code on your phone doesn't match theirs and they don't want to pick up. Fix by: Trying another time of day to call; when doing calls, document the last time you called in your CRM software or whatever you use to track your notes. Try a morning, an afternoon, and a night time because you don't know when your prospect is around.

Conversations but no meetings booked—This is either a script issue or execution of the script. The script might need to be modified, or the person performing the script might need more training.

Meetings are happening but no closes—The presentation is off, the closing process is off, the offer may be wrong, the salesperson may be offering the wrong thing to the wrong person, or the closer might not be following or using a script.

Call number goes down—Salespeople are slacking off, not managing time, wasting time, hiding, soothing emotional pain; they need to be amped up by a great meeting, coaching, or outside motivation.

Conversation number goes down—How old are the leads? Is it a holiday? Is it the wrong season or time of year? Are there people on vacation? Did lead quality go down? Is the marketing campaign either fished out or burned out?

Close numbers go down—Closer is off process and is improvising, needs retraining, coaching, and put back on the script.

Money collected goes down—Closers are accepting too many terms deals, not big enough deposits; need negotiation training to collect in full. Closers may be off script or off policy. Need an audit of closing.

You need to know your conversion percentages over time and your fishbowl will help you track that:

- percent of people who pick up the phone on call
- percent of people who convert into meetings
- percent of people who you close on meetings

These closing percentages are directly related to your skills and strategic ability to do your calls at the right time with the right script and execute the script in a professional way.

They key to success in running a professional sales practice is knowing your dollars per call and maintaining a strong "fishbowl" and sticking to your plan. If you can do those things, sales will become one of the most successful endeavors you have ever undertaken because you will see that the inputs certainly yield worthwhile outputs.

Top Performers Peak 3 Times a Year and the Pit Of Despair

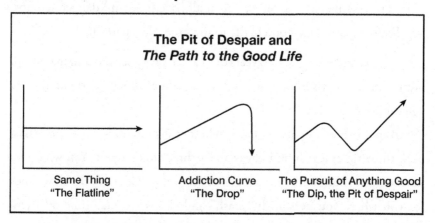

In life there are three choices to constantly make: what is easy vs. doing nothing vs. what is hard but good. As you make daily choices, there are three patterns that form:

1. **The Flatline**—every day is the same; no better, no worse. This is what happens when we get stuck in routine and things stay the same. This is where change needs to happen.
2. **The Drop**—The addiction curve. This is where things get better every day, little by little, until suddenly the floor falls out from under you.

Think about the smoking habit. Every day smoking gets better and better until one day you have lung cancer. Or eating a donut a day is a great idea until you have a heart attack. Things that feel good right away sometimes do not have great results over time.

3. **The Dip and the Pit of Despair**–Anything good in life goes through the dip. At the beginning, we feel a small hit of success, followed by a long, dangerous, and difficult trench called the dip. In the dip, the pit of despair is where most people quit. However, if you survive the pit, you will receive the rewards that are reserved for you on the other side of the dip. Typically, the better the reward, the longer and more dangerous the trench. Starting a business, having a family, or becoming a professional athlete or musician, all have long and dangerous dips. Typically, anything good in life follows the "dip" pattern.

In sales, usually the first two years of a career have a serious and major dip, but if you can survive five years, you will become affluent, and in ten years you can become rich.

Peak performers in any industry, whether it's athletics, acting, or sales, peak three times a year and have valleys three times a year. You would be wise to track your numbers throughout the year and identify the slow times for you where you personally "crash" and choose to take time off then. When the machine is off, it's totally off; when the machine is on, it's totally on. Embrace the peak times and harvest as much as you can, work ungodly hours to get a full yield, but then when the season changes and you have mapped out the times that are not as good, use those to recharge, retrain, reboot, and get ready for the next wave of greatness. When I wrote this book for you, I was in Costa Rica in one of the valley times in my business so that when I turn the machine back on, I come back recharged with new weapons to bring to the battlefield. Know when to use your uptime to the fullest and know when to rest to the fullest.

Brand/Marketing/Sales/Product Pyramid

As a salesperson it's important to know where you fit into the food chain of a company and how different departments affect the relative ease of a sale or difficulty of a sale. In general, the more difficult the product is to sell, like investments, financial advice, or raising capital, the higher skilled you must be and the commissions are higher. Especially if you have to constantly find your own leads. The company has taken the marketing money and given it to the salesperson in the form of commissions to bring business in the door instead of paying for marketing and this is a good thing for a skilled salesperson. On the flip side, if you work for a company where leads are handed to you every day, the commissions are lower, and the skill required is lower. The only upside is that your risk is less.

Typically, the harder it is to make the sale, the more you will get paid.

How to Make the Sale as Easy as Possible— Pyramid of Making a Successful Sale

Salespeople are arguably the most important people in every company: they are usually the highest paid, and when they are doing well, they are adored by executives no matter how unruly. But salespeople fit into the middle of the food chain of making a successful sale. Let's examine the Pyramid of Making a Successful Sale.

The pyramid is the strongest structure known to man and if you can get your ethics, product, sales department, marketing department, and branding to department to work together in a choreographed fashion, this is truly an unstoppable force of money. Let's examine the pyramid.

The Soil Beneath the Pyramid—Clean Ethics "Do What's Right for the Customer"

Usually people who remind you of how great their ethics are not as ethical as they say. To be truly powerful, you should not have to remind people, same with ethical people. When it comes to ethics, it's better to show it then to tell it. If you are a company who focuses on "Doing what's right for the customer no matter what," you will be golden in the ethics department. Take care of the customer and they will take care of you. You might make less money, you might make money slowly, but over time you are building trust with the customer and the marketplace. That will reap exponential dividends in the future and blossom into a great brand that can be trusted. Zappos, the legendary online shoe retailer who was bought out by Amazon was famous for having great ethics. If the salesperson didn't have the right shoes for the customer, the salesperson would research where the customer could get such shoes and send the customer straight to a competitor! You might be thinking, that's insane! But what happened in return was the customer was very likely to return and become a repeat customer after such a huge trust-building gesture.

Conversely, one of the greatest salespeople I have ever met in person is Jordan Belfort—the real Wolf of Wall Street, who stole hundreds of millions of dollars from investors due to his bad ethics. He and his company were purposely pushing junk investments into the hands of ultra-wealthy investors and taking obscene commissions knowing that the investments would never work out. This kind of "pump and dump" strategy will ruin your company, ruin your brand forever, and potentially put you in jail—like it did to Jordan, who lost everything. If he was a clean player, he would have made money slower, and over time could be a billionaire today, but instead he threw his ethics to the wind.

Even today, Jordan preaches on ethics, although it's hard to believe him—do people really change? That black mark will be on his brand forever, no matter how cool the movie the Wolf of Wall Street is. Jordan Belfort is anathema to some people simply because he failed to do what was right when he was young.

The foundation of the pyramid—A great product—"Does this thing actually work?"

Laid upon the soil of clean ethics is the strong foundation of the pyramid—the product. Your product only needs one thing. "Does this thing actually work?" Fortunately, the vast majority of products do work. They do what they claim to, and most companies live up to the claim they are selling. I have a small burger joint a few blocks from my office called "Cindy's Burgers." The brand is nothing, the marketing is nothing, the salespeople sometimes are unfriendly as per Trip Advisor Reviews online, but the food is amazing! The product is homemade Greek burgers and Greek food for a great price. Cindy doesn't need a salesperson because she has a great product; it does what it promises for a fair price, and that is where the development of that business stops: with the product.

The old adage is true: the product does sell itself, in some cases, like ice cream on a hot day or popcorn at a movie. But most companies do not have the luxury of selling ice cream on a hot day (especially in the wintertime), and that is why we need salespeople.

The base of the pyramid—The sales department—"What you say about you"

Built on the foundation of the pyramid is the sales department. Many companies actively "walk their customers over the finish line." That is why a great number of them employ salespeople. Salespeople and the sales presentation must coordinate with the ethics of the company, product department, marketing department and branding department to coordinate the most effective sales presentation. In today's world, it takes a coordinated effort and sales choreography to make complex and high-trust sales in a low-trust world.

What remains true is the power of scripting and sales choreography to create compelling sales situations where customers want to buy. Sales choreography is a multimedia sequence and mix of online and offline activity that creates optimum buying situations for customers so that it is "easy" for them to buy and they feel safe and secure doing so.

The goal of sales choreography is to ensure that very few leads, prospects, or customers end up in the endless "trash bin" of leads that are underworked or forgotten. Every company has a large "trash bin" of leads and previous customers that is under worked and underserved. The company has spent great resources acquiring through marketing efforts. Sales choreography is to extract the most value out of the leads as possible and build trust with the clients throughout the process.

The trouble with salespeople is that for generations, salespeople have been known by the public to "rip people off" and "be crooks" Building trust through salespeople alone can be a challenge because no matter what a salesperson says, the customer will always be distrusting in the beginning. We live in a world today where showing the customer the facts and the results is, and always will be, more powerful than anything a salesperson can ever say. Prospects will always be checking what salespeople say with a fine-tooth comb to make sure that no red flags are tripped or that the bullshit meter doesn't start to tip off the scale. It's harder to be a salesperson today more than ever because you are under more scrutiny more than ever.

The world is no longer buyer beware; it's now seller beware! The sales process must be systematized and scripted with a microscope to make sure it is done in the exact right way.

No matter what a salesperson says, it will always be challenged by the customer, either overtly or covertly in their mind, and that is where the marketing and branding departments come in.

The middle of the pyramid—The marketing department—"What you say about you"

There is an old saying: "If you have to sell, it's because your marketing sucks," and this statement is somewhat true. Companies with great marketing don't have to sell nearly as hard as companies with horrible marketing. Think of a store like Best Buy that sends out full-color flyers in neighborhoods filled with great marketing and great offers, and their store is full of people gobbling up electronics in their big box store, even in the age of e-commerce. Best Buy was so strong on their marketing that they in fact wiped out all other electronics retailers in Canada and are the last standing giant.

The marketing department is your chance to get your value and your promise out to the marketplace, but it is still mistrusted because again it's "what you say about you." There is no question that marketing is ultra-important for generating qualified leads for salespeople, and picking the right messages and media to attract those people, but at the end of the day, it will always fall short of making a sale on its own. Don't ignore the consumer-driven marketing that will spread like wildfire. The consumer drives the market.

The top of the pyramid—The branding department—"What others say about you"

"If you have to put out marketing, your brand sucks."

The top of the pyramid is the company's brand. The brand is the reputation, the relationship with the customers, the trust that has been formed over the years, and most importantly, "What others say about you."

What others say about you makes up your brand, and thus you never really own your brand; the public does. Apple computers has developed such a legendary brand that customers still line up outside the doors of the Apple store to get the hottest new gadget; who knows how long that will continue for? Apple was just in a class action lawsuit against them for purposely slowing down their products, so they could sell more under the leadership of Tim Cook. Would Steve Jobs the founder and CEO have done that? That destroys the ethics of the company and the integrity of the products—it will hurt the brand! "It takes a lifetime to build a great brand and five minutes to destroy it," to paraphrase the words of billionaire Warren Buffet, who invests in great brands and holds them for life.

If you have a great brand, you don't need to be a strong marketer, and you don't have to be a strong salesperson, because people simply buy. A great brand only happens when the ethics, the product, the salespeople, and the marketing align into the intangible value that comprise a great brand.

Donald Trump when running for president claimed he was worth $10 billion while *Forbes* and other sources showed his net worth between $2–4 billion, and my guess was that in Trump's mind, his brand will be worth $7 billion more after he's finished being president, as all presidents become much richer after finishing their term, but it's hard to place an exact value on a brand. Other sources have estimated that Trumps brand went down by $1 billion from all the lost business deals from the "things he said" but who knows? Brands are intangible assets that can be monetized into real assets.

Kylie Jenner, the youngest Kardashian, is set to become a billionaire in record time because of her fame and Instagram account, and she has sold hundreds of millions of dollars of her makeup line on brand alone. This is a perfect example of sales and marketing fame.

All of the departments of a company, the ethics, the product, the sales team, the marketing team, and the branding team should be working hard every day to build trust and brand equity in the marketplace to make it easier and easier to sell in the marketplace every day as market trust gets built.

The Right Marketing and the Right Leads

One of the keys to successful selling is to get in front of the right people. It's important to work closely with the marketing department to constantly be checking if "the leads are qualified."

You could be a stellar salesperson and sell nothing because the audience was wrong. I've learned this the hard way several times speaking and doing sales presentations to wrong audiences. Usually I can convert 15–30 percent of a room into sales and when I have tried some rooms, the sales are almost 0 percent. Same presentation, zero sales. If you do this too many times, you will lose your sales self-esteem.

Upon further investigation, the people in those rooms were made up of nonbuyers of my product or they did not fit my niche at all. It was a marketing error on my part to put myself in front of such audiences, and I should stick to the profile of my proven buyers.

The only side caveat to this is to have your product marked as the same product "but for seniors," "for real estate investors," "for speakers," "for financial planners," or whatever other niche you would wish to retarget. Everybody thinks they are different, and while this is a fallacy, still it's a true fallacy in every customers mind: my situation is different, my company is different, my industry is different, and my product is different. It is only in very rare cases that it is actually different. You must cater the message towards the niche and not assume your niche will cross over into theirs with proper "customer tailoring" to the audience.

No matter how good of salesperson you are, no matter how good the presentation, it will never work on the wrong audience. Work closely with your marketing team to ensure you are targeting the right leads.

Dress for Success—Three Seconds Buys You Thirty Seconds

They say that three seconds buys you thirty seconds, thirty seconds buys you two minutes, two minutes buys you half an hour, half an hour buys you two hours, and two hours will buy you a day. People don't buy you. They buy your image and your appearance and what it means to them.

Generally, the most effective salespeople want to appear to be the trusted advisor. "The doctor," in that niche, is there to diagnose and make an educated recommendation to their client. You must look the part, act the part, and dress the part. After all, if it looks like a duck, quacks like a duck, and walks like a duck, it must be a duck.

A good rule of thumb to follow is to be dressed one notch above your client. It communicates you are on the same level, but a little bit more professional, which they like to see. People get into rapport with professionals who are sharp as a tack, enthusiastic as hell, and an expert in their field. You must look it.

All of Life Is a Stage

Whatever role you are playing in the theatre of the prospect's mind, you must dress the way he would expect. The IBM executive look—dark navy suit, solid color tie, white shirt, black oxford shoes, black dress socks, no jewelry except maybe a wedding band, no facial hair, clean cut tightly cropped hair—is classic and is "ketchup" in that it goes with everything. This look works for positions of trust like real estate, financial, insurance, securities, banking, and funerals, and the more conservative the look, the better. You are not dressing for yourself; you are dressing to respect your customer and show them what they want to see. It doesn't matter if you're overdressed or dressed better than everyone else. Think about it. Why would you dress to "fit in" to a low expectation culture? Why not dress better than everyone else? Dressing for success means dressing a level up.

Conversely if you are a plumber, you need to look like a plumber. The word is congruence—"How does the look of this person align with the messages they are sending to me?" If the message and the look are incongruent, that sets off a red flag in the customer's mind.

Dressing for success is more about creating absolutely zero reasons why someone would not want to do business with you. When people meet you, they judge you as hard as they can. In kindergarten we are told not to judge other people, but we mercilessly judge them and place them into neat tidy boxes in our minds. If there is the slightest reason in appearance to not do business with you, you will already be at a disadvantage.

The Guide to Commanding Power with Your Appearance

The sculpture carved out of stone is not finished until there is nothing left to take away. The same goes for your appearance.

Generally offensive trust-killing decisions that can give you a negative appearance to the general population

WARNING: This list is NOT politically correct, but it will make you more money to eliminate the following items. if you are easily offended, move on to the next section.

Facial Hair—Generally any facial hair is perceived by others subconsciously to be psychological signal that you are hiding something. It is rare for first world leaders to have facial hair. Third world dictators have an assortment of moustaches and beards, and facial hair is associated with outlaws, pirates, etc. The only exception to this rule would be a neatly cropped moustache, which is actually proven to increase a man's earnings. Police, fire, military, and executives wear moustaches to appear more masculine. But if given a choice between no hair and hair, I say no hair every time.

Man rings—Anything more than a wedding ring is generally too much. A pinkie ring is scientifically proven to be trust killing in all cases unless you are a casino manager or a professional hustler. Rings are associated with gangs, bikers, pirates, criminals, etc.

The two-hand handshake—When you shake someone's hand, it is never in your interest to put your other hand on top of theirs; this is offensive across the board and will weaken your position.

Bad teeth or breath—Poor dental hygiene or breath can easily turn someone off. Smell goes straight to the emotional brain and the thinking brain doesn't even get a chance to think about it before the emotions say "no." If you have a bad breath, do a cleanse, go on a fast, or clean out your digestion because breath comes from the colon. Bad teeth make you appear lower class; the old adage holds true: "Dress British, think Yiddish, talk American." It's better to have gentlemanly teeth than a pirate's smile.

Poor grooming—Poor grooming is proven in all pack animals, chickens, dogs, cats, pigs, and even humans to be animals lower on the pecking order. The pecking order comes from chickens in which the alpha chickens will peck on the weaker chickens all the way down to the omega chicken that gets pecked the most.

It's proven that in the poorest ghettos and the poorest parts of sub-Saharan Africa that women will spend money on lipstick before they will spend money to feed their children. This places them higher on the pecking order and gives them a higher chance of attracting a mate. The same is true with men and women in the ghetto who spend all their money on sporty clothes and the newest Nike shoes. Being well groomed and well-dressed will place you as the alpha animal in the pack; the omega is always disheveled. No one wants to buy from the omega.

Dirty or wrinkled—If you are dirty or have wrinkled clothing, especially suits, it immediately places you in a negative light. Have enough suits so you can rotate them in and out of the dry cleaners and keep them looking fresh. All of this sends a nonverbal signal that you mind the details. Be intentional.

The smell of smoke—The smell of smoke is now taboo in the modern world, and some people gag when they smell it. If you are a smoker, quit.

It is a horrible habit anyways, there is no benefit, and it is just a sign of perpetual weakness.

Out of shape—Being out of shape shows you can't take care of yourself or you are working too hard, neither of which is attractive to your customer.

Many top performers do at least the bare minimum to stay in shape. Several very rich billionaires I have met hate exercise, but they still do the minimum because there is no way around it.

Sick looking—If you look sick, it places you as a weaker animal in the pack. No one wants to buy from a sick person. Mind your complexion and the health of your organs, because organ health will show up on a person's skin.

Ethnic distinctions outside of your ethnic niche—Anything you wear that is of a religious or ethnic preference—for example a turban—is perceived negative outside of its own ethnic community. In ethnic marketing, these ethnic distinctions work, but if you want to be outside the niche, eliminate it.

Your name—If you have a name that no one can say or spell, change it, especially if it's a very ethnic name. If you want to have the broadest appeal, you will need to pick a name with the broadest appeal. Many very famous and successful people have changed their names. My name Stefan Aarnio is a horrible name because no one can say it or spell it, but it is Western enough that people think it's Italian, and it's unique on Google. I own everything "Stefan Aarnio," so I use it as an asset online.

Accents—Accents are negative across the board. Take a class to eliminate your accent. I understand that you can never fully eliminate it, but several successful people have eliminated their accents like Gene Simmons of Kiss who speaks five languages. His first language is not English, and he grew up in New York, but chose to sound the "way they sound on the news" so he does not have a Yiddish accent and does not have a New York accent; instead, he chose the most marketable one.

Tattoos—You may love your tattoos, you may hate them, but cover them or have them removed. If you are selling Harley Davidson motorcycles maybe it's okay to have tattoos or if you are a rock star in a mega band like

Guns and Roses, sure, but tattoos show a sign of weakness. Companies like Disney have a "no tattoo" policy, and they are right. The general public does not want to see tattoos. In Japan you can't enter a public pool or show a tattoo in public because it is a sign of gangs and the Yakuza. If you are thinking of getting a tattoo, please don't.

Anything on a female salesperson that sexualizes her—Females in selling and business will probably always have an uphill battle selling to male clients. The reason for this is, many men view women as wives, mothers, sisters, girlfriends, and mistresses. If there is anything on a female's appearance like "too much leg," cleavage, or anything that makes her sexy, she will be taken less seriously. Even female shoes are sexualized and Chinese culture uses sexual foot bindings. Wear conservative everything and if in doubt, go more conservative.

Too much female jewelry—Too much jewelry sexualizes and cheapens a woman in business. Unless you are a gypsy belly dancer, wear the bare minimum and keep it conservative to get respect.

Unpolished shoes—If you have shoes that should be polished, get them polished and keep them polished. Polish your shoes before you leave the house; it's a sign of social status and gentlemanliness. Have a large enough rotation of shoes so that you if you are short on time you can take pre-polished shoes.

Posture—Good athletic posture, straight back, shoulders back, full of health and vigor is what a buyer wants to see. Bad posture is a sign of disrespect and is negative.

Speech impediments—If you have a speech impediment, work with a professional to get rid of it; it won't help you sell.

The deal-signing pen—The last line of resistance on the deal is the pen you pull out to ink the contract. Have a nice, beautiful pen that communicates trust and that this is the "right choice." A good rule of thumb is go to a pen dealer and get a starter luxury pen from Mont Blanc, Cross, Visconti, or some other brand. It helps seal the deal and tells a good story in the buyer's mind.

Your notebook—Have a presentable looking notebook with you that communicates class. I use *The Black Book Journal* and *The High Performance Journal*. You can order them online if you wish to have a nice notebook for meetings and personal organization.

Your bag or briefcase—Have something of class that makes sense for your position. When it comes to bags, a good leather bag will last years and send a positive professional message. A doctor carries a black leather bag to house calls; you should have the equivalent of that. The first nice black leather briefcase I had was made by Coach, was beautiful, and served me for years. I now use a roller luggage briefcase as I am traveling and presenting almost every week. Have a bag that communicates professionalism.

DISC—Four Types of Salespeople: Your Personality and Balancing Yourself Out

There are four types of people: those who want to be liked, those who want to be comfortable, those who want to be right, and those who want to win. There have always been four archetypes of human personalities dating back to the Greeks when they would describe people as earth, fire, wind, water. DISC is an industrial psychological test that classifies people into four categories: Dominance—those who want to win, Influence—those who want to be liked, Compliance—those who want to be right, and Submission—those who want to be comfortable. There are several names that have been used for the same four personalities, but they usually start with the letters D, I, S, and C.

As far as business partners and love partners you are always attracted to the diagonal position on the chart. Dominance goes with Submission and Influence goes with Compliance. There is another section in this book about how this four-personality system applies to customers and how to handle them, but this section is for the purposes of understanding yourself and your own communication style.

As a rule, we usually have a primary profile. For myself I am a D first, I second. As far as developing my own personality, I need to learn my opposites to become a well-rounded salesperson.

Dominance without any Submission becomes
punishing to for the customer to deal with.

Submission without any Dominance becomes too soft and can't close.

Influence without Compliance becomes shallow, flashy,
with no substance or product knowledge.

Compliance without Influence becomes lost in the details and
specs of the product and loses the customer altogether.

They say that when a man marries a woman he marries his complement, and he is supposed to assimilate some of her traits and she assimilates some of his. This is old ancient wisdom and usually men become better and more productive after getting married and having kids. Perhaps it's the time spent adopting the opposite traits that round them out? Or perhaps it's because he has an accountability partner every night checking on him also known as his wife? Or perhaps it's because he has a strong "Why" to succeed, usually his children and their wellbeing?

Working on your opposite traits is major to your growth as a salesperson and ability to be hard enough, soft enough, have enough information, and enough sizzle to sell to all types.

Framing, Frames, and Counters

In Oren Klaff's book, *Pitch Anything*, the author outlines the use of "frames." Frames are simply the version of reality that you generate for yourself. Each person creates a frame with their own version of reality, and when two frames collide, one frame will overtake the other.

For example, two alpha males will collide with a power frame, and both will seek dominance. In the end, one will take the alpha position and one the beta position. They might defy one another to attempt for dominance, but eventually one will become the alpha and the other will be the beta. This analogy is important when understanding the psychology of the sale.

Types of frames you can use to control the reality around the sale:

Power Framing—To create a power frame is to take dominance and control over the situation. Powerful people will create power for themselves by having a receptionist and waiting room. They will place a tiny little chair for the customer across from a large mahogany desk and a powerful chair for themselves.

This creates power for them and establishes them as the alpha while you are stuck in the beta trap. **The counter to a power frame is to defy the trappings of power.** When they offer you a patronizing glass of water in the waiting room, refuse. When the boss makes you sit in the little chair, prefer to stand. These small acts of defiance can help you take power and control in the situation. On the flip side, there are times when it makes sense to fit into the narrative of power and never forget the first law of power in Robert Greene's forty-eight laws of power: "Don't outshine the master."

Time Framing—Time framing is to take control of the time in a sales situation. When the client says he only has thirty minutes, tell him you will be done in fifteen. Control the time, set the times, and keep them short to remain powerful in the transaction.

Setting a timer at the beginning of your pitch is a very powerful way to show integrity and that you respect the other side's time. Amateurs ramble on and on. Pros are succinct. Control the time of the sale; it adds to your power. The counter to time frame is to cut the time of the other side shorter: if he wants fifteen minutes, give him five; this will put you in control of the time.

Prize Framing—You are the prize, or your offer is the prize. The customer may think that their money is the prize, and it's your job as a salesperson to flip around the value for money equation. Making your offer exclusive, making you exclusive, making what you offer scarce or one of a kind flips the money for value equation on its head. Their money is no longer the prize; your offer is the prize. If you fail to prize frame you and your product, the customer will always think that their money is the prize to be won and you are of lower value.

Analyst Framing—Sometimes your customers, when barraged with data will slip into an analyst frame. An analyst frame is where thinking and numbers take over and the prospect has to "think about it," "run the numbers," or "do some due diligence."

The analyst frame is death to all decision making as the neocortex, the thinking brain, is unable to make decisions. Decisions are made with emotions and more so the reptile brain, which operates on fear and greed. To get your prospect out of an analyst frame, get them into a story that will bring them into the emotional brain and shut off the "thinking brain" that is killing their decision-making power.

Decision Making—How Buyers Make Decisions—Three Parts to the Human Brain

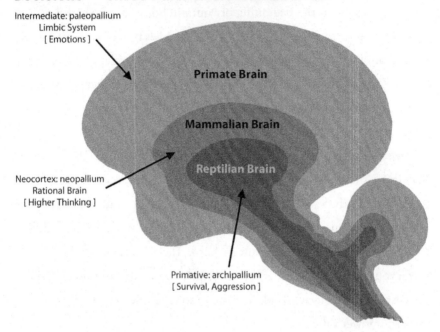

Intermediate: paleopallium
Limbic System
[Emotions]

Primate Brain

Mammalian Brain

Reptilian Brain

Neocortex: neopallium
Rational Brain
[Higher Thinking]

Primitive: archipallium
[Survival, Aggression]

The human brain is not one entity, but rather three entities stacked upon one another. The brain is divided into three somewhat independent smaller brains and to understand how people make real buying decisions, you must understand all three brains.

The Neocortex—The last part of the human brain to evolve was the neocortex. This part of the brain is the "thinking" brain that can imagine the future, see into the past, sing songs, write poetry, paint beautiful pictures, write books, and lie, cheat, and steal. This part of the brain is the "let me think about it brain." The neocortex can think forever, but it can never make a decision. Decisions are made in the emotional brain and action is taken in the reptile brain. The neocortex is a trap for you as a salesperson because the last thing you want is your prospects thinking and unable to make a decision. You must tailor your presentations so that they run on emotions, fear, and greed to avoid getting stuck in the disabled "thinking brain." A confused mind never buys, and neither does a thinking mind. The neocortex cannot ever make a decision.

The Mammalian Brain—The mammalian brain is that part of the brain that fights, flees, flocks, or freezes. It controls the emotions and is a main influencer on buying decisions. People do not buy on logic, ever. They always buy on emotions and justify with logic after the fact. The main emotion you want your prospects to feel throughout your presentation is the "yes" feeling that keeps you in rapport.

The main emotion you want them to avoid is the "no" feeling, which may be linked to disgust or other offensive emotions and will break rapport instantly. Tailor your presentation to eliminate anything that will give your prospects the "no" feeling so that the presentation is a series of "yesses" followed by a trial close and a close.

Some studies have shown that the emotional brain carries on through the digestive tract right into the stomach and the colon. Some people theorize that prolonged states of fear and anxiety are what create stomach ulcers and gastrointestinal ulcers as the emotional brain carries on down through the gut and intestines. This is why people say, "go with your gut" as your gut contains very old decision-making equipment that must have been useful in earlier times. No matter how advanced people and technology become, we will always make decisions with our "gut" and this is why salespeople are so valuable. People want someone they trust to walk them over the finish line and people will pay a premium through a sales commission to feel good throughout the process.

The Reptile Brain—The reptilian brain controls the limbic system and is the oldest part of the brain. This brain operates on fear and greed only. This brain has the strongest decision-making power and holds nearly all of the action taking power over the body. Your prospect must feel significant "greedy" gain over your offer, but "fear of loss" can also be a huge motivator for the reptile brain to take action. It may sadden you to know that humans make decisions based on fear and greed, but do not be saddened by this information. Instead, embrace the mechanics of the mind and use this information to communicate your offer in such a way that will appeal to the reptilian brain that controls all action over the body.

The Power of Scripting and Sales Choreography

"A business absolutely devoted to service will have only one
worry about profits. They will be embarrassingly large."
—Henry Ford

Stop selling and start serving: A service-focused sales choreography is the difference between having your customers happy to hear from you and loving the buying process versus an adversarial, distrustful, negotiation process with haggling over price and terms. Focus on the customer, devote yourself to service, and do not worry about the profits: service first, profits second.

The sales process is easier now for some industries and harder for others. Technology has shortened the sales process for many in the modern world with social media, the internet and technology yet to come—which will likely include artificial intelligence and virtual reality!

All of this is making the sales process in many ways longer and more complicated in some industries and shorter and easier in others.

What remains true is the power of scripting and sales choreography to create compelling sales situations where customers want to buy. Sales choreography is a multimedia sequence and mix of online and offline activity that creates optimum buying situations for customers so that it is "easy" for them to buy and they feel safe and secure doing so.

Some of the elements you may use in sales choreography are:

Online ads to lead capture offers—Many sales processes and funnels today start with an online ad and online lead capture offer, also known as bait: something offered for free in exchange for the customer's contact information. This exchange of information for value is of great value to a sales team as it generates fresh qualified leads for offline follow up and can be done relatively cheaply on a consistent basis.

Online application forms—You may offer an opportunity for clients to apply for your product online if it's a more complex product to sell and clients need to be qualified.

Free reports, e-books, real books as loss leaders—Offering free information by way of free reports, e-books, or real books in the mail as loss leaders positions your sales team as a knowledgeable choice in your industry. A published 50,000-word book is one of the most powerful sales tools ever and will prove your knowledge over your competition who do not have the resources to publish such an advanced tool.

White papers (printed)—Case studies of successful customers who have been served and are happy with your offer. These are the second most influential pieces of sales literature that customers are seeking after published books. White papers are expensive and take time to generate, so again, several of your competitors will not have such a document. A simple title like "The types of people we serve:" followed by a laundry list of demographics that "think they are different" will dispel the "I'm different objection" that every buyer falsely has placed in his mind.

Webinars—Either a live or recorded informational session followed by a sale is a great way to 1) educate buyers but also ask for business and 2) make sales. Webinars save travel time and costs and therefore are very convenient ways to reach several customers. The downside is they are not as powerful as real live seminars, but the savings on cost make them a popular choice for several sales and marketing teams. It is a great way to continue to provide content, and they can also be prerecorded to be consumed at any time of day by any customer.

Online Videos—Video is becoming more and more competitive for buyers in the modern world. Good production quality and sound quality is expected nowadays to create trust. Video is getting more competitive every day and it is also becoming one of the favorite ways for people to buy things as sites like YouTube become more and more competitive.

Live Stream—Several social media services are offering live streaming services direct to the customer's eyeballs. This is an increasingly powerful tool for making online sales or educating and interacting with live customers.

Infomercials—Infomercials are still powerful sale tools even though TV viewership is precipitously trending down. Infomercials are moving online and still sell products where prospects need to be educated to buy.

Live Seminars—A live seminar where the customer is receiving education on complex or high trust products like education are always a favorite way for customers to "try before they buy." Live seminars build major trust and although they are fraught with horrendous expenses, people are willing to spend tens of thousands of dollars at live seminars because they can feel the trust and bond between the speaker, the message and themselves. Churches around the world hold live seminars and collect billions of dollars to save souls. Take a hint from the church; they know how to sell and collect money.

Glossy Brochures—Although glossy brochures often are not enough for a customer to buy, they still like to hold the information in their hands. Having a glossy looking brochure is a great reference tool in a sales presentation and a great way to show value in a tangible way. You cannot escape the glossy brochure in the modern world, and buyers still want and expect them.

Workbooks—A workbook that the customer can work through to become educated over a two- or three-day seminar can be unbelievable powerful to create trust and make the customer feel like he is learning. Workbooks create an educational environment and show that your team cares and is organized and committed to helping your customer make the right decisions.

Sample Materials/Sample Products—Everyone loves free samples and free products. When you can offer samples, customers can "feel" the product for themselves and make a decision based on their feelings.

Free Demos—Test drives are still popular at car dealerships because people want a live demonstration of how the product works. Free demos dispel the objection "does this thing really work"? which creates power for your team.

Emails—Emails are a weak form of communication, but people still expect them and still read them. Your sales choreography will likely use email in some form to confirm orders and appointments.

Text Messages—A more powerful way of reaching a customer are text messages because they are rarely ignored, vibrate, and go straight into a buyer's pocket via a cell phone. These are great for sending reminders into your sales meetings.

Free Gifts—A gift of chocolate, brownies, or cookies that are unrelated to the sale you are making can really boost trust. Free lunches or cookies can also make people feel comfortable.

Live Promo Events—Live promotional events on site can be very powerful ways to sell things that have to be "seen to be believed." They also create a party atmosphere and "fun" around your company to make people want to buy.

Newsletters (printed)—Newsletters are a great way to infiltrate your customer's inbox every month with useful information. They also are seen to be higher value than email or electronic communication.

Blogs—Blogs are still fantastic for gaining SEO rankings and making yourself an expert online. Customers still like to read blogs to make them feel comfortable about working with you, and they are a great way to create return traffic to your website.

Video Series—An educational video series online can be a great way to nurture a relationship where clients have to "build trust over time." In some industries people will not want to buy until they have seen hours and hours of your educational content. Video series can deliver value over time to marinate customers into trust and buying positions.

CDs or DVDs in the Mail—Believe it or not, people still like receiving old media like CDs and DVDs in the mail because it feels like a present and the physicality of the information makes it seem more important than an online video.

Postcards—Glossy post cards with reminders and notes, especially if hand written can be great ways to invite customers to take action on the next step of your offer.

Handwritten Notes—These are very powerful to send in the mail as they show you care and took the time for the personal touch.

Snail Mail Letters—A letter from the founder, or a letter from the sales agent, hand signed can be very powerful ways to send sincere messages and sincere offers.

Multi Salesperson Meetings—Some sales processes will involve several salespeople and a series of meetings. Salespeople can be rotated until the right personality match is found or it could be a "setter/closer" type of sales relationship, but several sales nowadays require a rotation of salespeople to close, especially if it's a high trust sale.

Free Coaching Session/Consult/Strategy Session—A free one-on-one educational session followed by an offer from the person giving the lesson can be a great way to sell training, education, or other high trust offers.

Next Visit Offer—An offer for the next visit to the store or e-store is a very popular hook in e-commerce to reengage the prospect into a second or third sale.

Podcasts—These are a great ways to educate and create celebrity on your salesforce. Podcasts can add tremendous value for those who love to listen to them.

Building Your Sales Funnel and Sales Choreography

The sales and marketing teams must choose and choreograph the elements above to create the most optimum sales and buying situations possible. Each and every method above has a cost of time, effort, energy, and money, and you will need to figure out which pieces are most valuable to your customers and your process.

The sales process can be more convoluted today than ever before because customers can go online to your competitor in a fraction of a second and in fact, your company and several others are likely directly targeting the same people online. Having a stronger and better sales choreography, a better "show" to entertain and educate your buyers will always give you an edge in creating optimum buying situations for your buyers.

The Law of Averages: A Segmented Look At Types of Buyers

Not everyone is sellable. In fact, there is a small fraction of the population—5 percent of prospects—that are apathetic buyers. When you encounter these people, identify them as quickly as possible and do not waste your time trying to save someone who is hopelessly negative, apathetic, or simply uninterested. These people will destroy your self-esteem and tire you out. When you find an unsellable apathetic buyer, thank them for coming in and let them reach back out to you. Do not waste time on them, move on.

The self-actualizing buyer—5 percent of the population is the self-actu-alizing buyer; these people know what they need and what they want. They walk into the appropriate store and buy it. They are the dream customer and easy to work with. When you meet one of these people, make it easy for them to buy: make the sale and move on. Realize that they bought not because of your sales skills, but because they were self-actualized and knew what they wanted.

The 90 percent bulk of sellable buyers—90 percent of your prospects are sellable with some skill; some are ready to buy now, and some are ready to buy later and need to be followed up with. Overall, most people are sellable; the question becomes which ones can be sold today or closest to today, and which ones need to be nurtured into future sales.

Inside of this subsection of buyers are:

Buyers in heat—10–20 percent of your prospects are buyers in heat who are ready to buy right now. They have a need, a pain, and need to solve it now. Your job is to locate these people and write the order as quickly as possible. They will either buy from you or a competitor, but they are ready to buy!

Buyers in power—30–40 percent of your prospects are buyers in power. They want to buy, but maybe not today; they are not in pain and are instead in power, and your job is to present your offer in its best light, make a pro-posal, and find out when they will be making a decision and when the best time to revisit them is. They may be window shopping today, but they are serious and will make a purchase in the future. Never look at a sale as merely transactional. I've had people come back to me years after I first sold them, or talked to them, to purchase something.

Lookie Loos—30–40 percent These people are not serious and just curious; locate them as quickly as you can and eliminate them from your schedule. These people are professional time wasters who may appear to be buyers in power. You need to have a system to weed out the lookie loos and cut them off from wasting all of your precious time.

Four signs you are talking to a lookie loo:

1. They ask questions they seem to already know the answer to
2. They kick tires to the point of overkicking them
3. They appear to be over interested with too many oo's and aah's and yup's
4. When it comes to money and finances, they become vague or overconfident

The mistakes—These people were dragged into your funnel by someone else, maybe a spouse or a business partner and have no interest in ever buying. Locate them and eliminate them from your funnel so you do not waste time on them.

Hierarchy of Sales Skills Retail—Biz Sales

Not all salespeople are created equally. There is a hierarchy of salespeople and sales skills, and showing off the categories of different salespeople can give you an idea of the skills and experience that each level of selling has. Of course, anyone can train to make sales at a higher level, but when building a sales team with people from all different backgrounds, you can use this section to determine the skill level of other people's sales experience.

Low Skill Sales

Retail is where many salespeople can start their careers, and for many it can be a good place to start. Retail sales is typically low skill because the company you work for supplies leads through a store or a sales floor. The customer walks in ready to buy, and prospecting is minimal. The retail sales floor is usually set up to create an optimal selling environment, and there are usually heavy marketing expenditures to fill up the sales environment with customers.

All of these factors make retail sales a low-skill game relative to the other forms of selling, and thus retail sales are usually one of lowest paid, lowest skill positions available in sales. Commissions are usually around 1–2 percent and minimum wage. If you want more money, you will need to get into a more difficult environment where the company does not hand you leads every day. Salespeople always get paid less when the company is paying for the leads. Bring your own leads or your own book of business in one of the higher skill games to get paid the big dollars.

Low Medium Skills

Door-to-Door Sales—These are another place where salespeople start their careers. Door-to-door companies do not supply leads to their salespeople and thus, door to door is higher skill and higher paid than retail sales. Door-to-door sales usually have short pitches and simple offers that people can understand in a matter of minutes. This is the first opportunity to really make a career out of selling is once you take control of your own lead flow.

Medium Skill Sales

Corporate Sales and B2B Sales—Medium skills give you medium pay in corporate sales and B2B. B2B and corporate is somewhat easier than the super high skill sales because you work for a large company with a good training program, and typically the large companies have established offerings and good brand recognition.

In addition, several companies you are selling to have set budgets for your products and services and are "buying anyways." You may be convincing your customers to switch service providers, but the money is being spent anyways. That means there is more skill required in longer sales cycles and more gate keepers and committees to go through to get to the top, all of this extra work is compensated usually with generous corporate compensation packages plus commissions and benefits.

High Skill Sales

Business Sales, Biz Op Sales, Entrepreneurial Sales, Raising Capital— The highest skill game of sales is selling things that don't really exist. Selling businesses from one owner to another is an extremely challenging sale. Selling business opportunities like franchises is another high skill sale. Entrepreneurial sales for new companies and ideas and raising capital also fit into this model, and these are the highest paid and highest skill sales opportunities around. People who can master the high skill sale are the highest earners in the world and also the most skilled salespeople around. Aspire to be in the high skill category one day and watch your income grow exponentially.

The Purpose of a Salesperson

Your #1 job as a salesperson is to get a decision out of the prospect. There are five outcomes of any sales presentation and they are:

1. Yes
2. Yes, with a condition
3. Maybe
4. No, with a condition
5. No

You need to make it clear to your prospects that you are looking for a clear yes or no answer and that maybe is unacceptable because it means you didn't do your job very well. Contrary to popular belief, the #1 function of a salesperson is not to sell, but rather, show the value, determine if your value is a fit with the customer, and get a firm yes or no decision. A no decision is completely fine, and you need to embrace "the no" especially if it's not a fit. You are not looking for any customer for your product or service; rather, you are looking for the right customer to ethically sell to the right way.

Never sell your customer something he doesn't need, cannot use; qualify well, and disqualify as well. Your career will be long lived and very profitable if you allow "no" to be one of the outcomes. Welcome it and embrace it, especially on the wrong customers. Nothing strengthens your power position like "forcing a no" on a customer that you know is wrong for the product.

If it's not a fit, tell the customer up front and you will automatically go to #1 in trust in the customer's eyes because of your honesty and commitment to excellence in ethics. That is a client for life.

Top Three Traits of a Top Salesperson

There is a myth in the world of sales that there is such thing as a "natural" salesperson and you are either a "natural" or you are not. I believe this is a myth, but that surely there are people who may naturally be suited to sales. What are your core personality traits?

We've all seen people who seem natural at sales. They thrive in the sales environment.

Their personality is perceived to be more extroverted, or maybe they enjoy being with people, or maybe they enjoy presenting, but all of those traits to do not make a natural salesperson and can in fact turn into weaknesses down the road. Natural extroverts talk too much and can kill the sale. People who enjoy socializing can be inefficient and shallow and get nothing done while socializing too much. People who enjoy presenting may be horrible closers. Introverts make great listeners and possess many traits that are perceived to be "less desirable" as salespeople. However those traits can be developed into strengths.

What remains true is that all top performing salespeople have three traits in common: ego, empathy, and passion. Everything else—the technique, the mechanics, the delivery—can be learned through training.

e·go

ˈēgō/

noun

1.   a person's sense of self-esteem or self-importance.
"a boost to my ego"
synonyms: self-esteem, self-importance, self-worth, self-respect, self-
image, self-confidence
"the defeat was a bruise to his ego"

Top Sales Trait #1: Ego—Ego is what you think of yourself. It's the force that says "I am," and ego is important as a salesperson because you are required to go into the world, be unreasonable, make progress, and ultimately "push" on the world. When you push on the world, the world pushes back. Your ego is what will allow you to know your value, face rejection, and keep going despite the emotional pain that salespeople experience every day. After all, it's not water that sinks ships, but only when the water gets inside the hull of the boat does the boat start to sink. The same is true for the ego: if you allow negativity to penetrate your ego, you will sink. Your ego will allow you to "float" much like a boat in the face of adversity. A caution on the ego, however, is to not have too much. Too much ego is a turnoff and will make you blind in decision making. You must have enough ego to do your job but not so much that it ruins your relationships around you.

em·pa·thy
ˈempəTHē/
noun
noun: **empathy**
the ability to understand and share the feelings of another.

Top Sales Trait #2: Empathy—Zig Ziglar famously used to say, "They don't care about how much you know until they know how much you care." Understanding the feelings of your prospect is probably one of the most desired traits for buyers when meeting salespeople. People want to buy from people who "understand them" and understand their feelings, fears, and weaknesses. People buy out of need or want, and because both are positions of weakness, people fear being taken advantage of in almost every business situation.

Human nature is dark, and humans have been preying on weaker humans since the dawn of time. Empathy is a way to show your customers that you care about them and their wellbeing and want them to be treated fairly when dealing with you. Top salespeople can almost "feel" the emotions of their prospects intuitively and act like a mind reader because they are so in tune with feeling the emotions and psychic energy of their customer. This power comes from taking a genuine interest in people and focusing deeply on them and not yourself. The trait of empathy is hard to learn and harder to master, but if you can master empathy and combine it with healthy dose of assertiveness, you will be a top salesperson almost immediately.

pas·sion
ˈpaSHən/
noun
1.   strong and barely controllable emotion.
"a man of impetuous passion"

Top Sales Trait #3: Passion—A deep religious-like passion about your company and product is infectious and exciting to you and the people around you. When you use your product, love your product, love the company you are working for, and show intense love and passion for what you are selling. It's almost unstoppable in the face of a prospect because it is real.

Sales is simply the transfer of emotion, after all, and the deeper your love for your product and passion for your product, the more unstoppable you become in the face of objections. To become ultra-passionate about your product—buy it! Own it! Use it! Use it every day!

If you are a user yourself, you can sell your product with the undying belief that it works. Every prospect has the fear in their mind, "Does this thing actually work?" When you are living proof that the product is every word as good as you say it is, it's hard to deny the truth, especially a passionate deliverer of truth. You must own what you sell, if you sell cars you can't ride the bus to work. If you sell real estate, you can't be a renter.

If you sell insurance, you must own the maximum amount. Nothing will make you sell more or sell harder than you are becoming a passionate owner of your own product. If you fall out of love with your product one day, you must revisit your product from a place of gratitude and make a list of the twenty things that you "love" about your product. You must fall in love again and practicing gratitude is the way back into positivity and into love. Look yourself in the mirror and read the twenty things that you love while staring yourself in the face, making intense eye contact. You will fall in love again; sometimes you just need to be reminded of the greatness that you once saw inside of your product and reignite the passion.

What holds you back from your sales potential?
Fears/weaknesses/knowledge
Advice from a $100,000,000 man

Years ago, I met a man and he mentioned that five years from now we would all be in the same spot we are today and no closer to our potential unless we focused on three things. He proceeded to draw a diagram of a triangle as an iceberg floating in water. With his marker he divided the tip of the iceberg as 2 percent of what holds us back from our potential and under the waterline on the iceberg he divided the remainder of the iceberg into 49 percent and 49 percent. "You see?" he said, "what holds us back in life is only 2 percent knowledge, what you learn, what you know, your education, which, in the end isn't a huge factor. But what becomes huge in holding you back from your potential are your fears and your weaknesses."

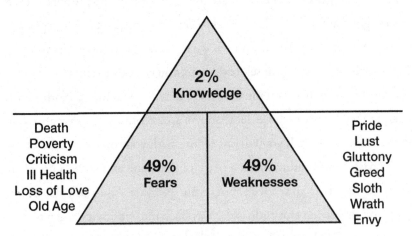

Knowledge - Fears - Weakness
Maximizes Knowledge, Minimizes Fears and Weaknesses

He went on to list the six ghosts of fear from Napoleon Hill's *Think and Grow Rich* and the seven deadly sins as per most religions of the world and explained how it was not our knowledge, but rather human fears and weaknesses that held us back from reaching our full potential as business people.

FEARs are nothing but False Evidence Appearing Real, and all fear exists in the mind. To transform the mind from fear into faith, I would say replace the word "fear" with the word "uncertainty." Everyone has natural uncertainties. Rather than feeling fear, explore what you are uncertain about. The mind cannot solve fear, but it can solve uncertainty and a lack of knowledge in any specific area. The six major human fears are illustrated below in the *Six Ghosts of Fear* by Napoleon Hill:

Six Ghosts of Fear

1. **Fear of death**—The mother of all fears and the ultimate unknown in life.
2. **Fear of failure**—Will keep a salesperson from taking new risks.
3. **Fear of Poverty**—The fear of losing money or being left in a worse financial position after taking a career in sales, a career with the risk of making no money through a commission structure. Many novice salespeople fear the idea of commission because of the potential downside of "making no money." This fear must be tamed as quickly as possible by breaking a sales day down into predicable actions with predictable results that generate predictable amounts of money over time.
4. **Feat of ill health**—This fear runs in parallel with fear of poverty, which leads to ill health. To be afraid of being sick will lower the power of your immune system and make you sick in turn. To be a top salesperson you need to display a degree of vitality and good health to be effective.
5. **Fear of loss of love**—Fear of losing your mate due to bad decisions.

6. **Fear of criticism**—Fear of being criticized for asserting your position in life.

None of these fears are real and all are perceived. Often the emotion of fear is more debilitating and damaging to the human body than the thing you fear happening. The opposite of fear is faith, the faith that "this will all work out." Many superstar salespeople practice a religion to practice the emotion of faith, giving them the spiritual power to overcome their fears and face the adversity within. I always recommend someone in the pursuit of money, success, fame, or fortune to take on a religion for study of the power of faith and to increase their spiritual power. Making money, after all, is a spiritual endeavor, and money is a spiritual energy unto itself. It comes from an idea backed by confidence, and faith is a wellspring from which confidence can be drawn. Without faith, one's mind will turn to fear, and if you are in fear long enough, fear will consume even the best of minds.

Weaknesses—Our weaknesses rob us of our energy and focus to be successful in any pursuit including a successful career in sales. Although this is not a book on religion, all religions of the world agree that sin is a waste of energy. All human weaknesses can be categorized by the seven deadly sins:

Seven Deadly Sins

1. **Pride**—The mother of all sins and the thinking that you are better or that your situation is different. You are no better or worse than anyone else, and your situation is never *really* different. This is pride talking, and pride is the most damaging of all human sins because it opens the door to the other six wastes of energy on the list.

2. **Greed**—The human emotion of wanting "more." Every human being has a magic number when it comes to money and material wealth, and that number is always "more." The most important question you have

in a sales career is when is "enough, enough?" Many professional sales-people do not sell for the money, but rather to serve in a big way. If you are driven by pure greed all the time, you will simply stop selling when you have a little bit of money. If you are driven by service and deliver-ing maximum service to the world, you will become rich beyond your wildest dreams because there is no limit to the amount of service one can give, and in fact, limitless service means limitless money.

3. **Lust**—The undisciplined emotion of sex in a negotiation is a pit-fall that can ruin many otherwise competent salespeople. Very often young single men and women can waste decades chasing members of the opposite (or same) sex around every night and every weekend and expend inordinate amounts of energy and throwing all the precious, valuable, actionable energy straight down the drain. A focus on sex can take an otherwise competent salesperson and take his eyes off the ball. Many young people end up taming their sexual urges by either being married or by being single and celibate. Napoleon Hill talks about sex transmutation in his book *Think and Grow Rich* that is transmuting sexual desire into creativity and ultimately great riches. You can choose to harness this energy to serve you, or it can become a destructive force in your life; it's up to you.

4. **Envy**—The desire to count the money of someone else will always destroy you. Don't focus on what other people have; focus on yourself and what you have. There is nothing more evil than desiring something that you have not earned. You will only ever really keep things in your life that you earn because anything given to you in life will be merci-lessly taken back by life if you do not earn the right to have it. This goes for having a beautiful body, a beautiful mind, money in the bank, lov-ing relationships, and anything else in life that is of true value. Only by earning real value do we appreciate value, and can we hold onto value.

Desiring things we do not earn through the function of envy is pure evil and a waste of energy.

5. **Wrath**—When emotions go up, intelligence goes down. Sometimes salespeople can get heated or frustrated, and they can let anger take over. When anger takes over, your chances of winning in a career in sales will drop to nearly 0 percent. Anger and wrath are generally a waste of energy, and you are best to "feel the emotion," understand why you feel it, acknowledge the emotion, and let it go. Forgiveness is a powerful emotion to release you of what you feel; you may think forgiveness is something you do for someone else, but rather it is something you do for yourself for emotional release.

6. **Sloth**—The art of selling takes a lot of work, time, effort, energy, and sometimes money to carry out. Many humans avoid selling purely because it takes energy—don't be lazy! Everything good in life will take an inordinate expenditure of energy, including getting in shape, earning money, having a loving relationship, and growing as a person. It all takes energy, and the time and energy are getting used up every day. Use your energy on something worthwhile. Dedicate your life to a worthwhile cause because you will die one day anyways, out of time and out of energy. You might as well choose something worthwhile to spend it all on.

7. **Gluttony**—The human emotion of anything done to the extreme. Gluttony is usually extreme overeating, extreme overdrinking, and taking anything to an extreme. Eating and drinking are necessary for life, but anything that is good will, in extreme excess, turn destructive and into a waste of energy. Sometimes salespeople can feel like the hare in the ancient fable "the tortoise and the hare" but you are always better off to be slow and steady and win over time. Very seldom can you be successful in life by being extreme all the time.

The common law of business balance:
Close as the lowest risk bidder, never lowest cost.

> *"Common Law of Business Balance—There is hardly anything in the world that someone cannot make a little worse and sell a little cheaper, and the people who consider price alone are that person's lawful prey. It's unwise to pay too much, but it's worse to pay too little. When you pay too much, you lose a little money—that is all. When you pay too little, you sometimes lose everything, because the thing you bought was incapable of doing the thing it was bought to do. **The common law of business balance prohibits paying a little and getting a lot**—it can't be done. If you deal with the lowest bidder, it is well to add something for the risk you run, and if you do that you will have enough to pay for something better."*
>
> *—John Ruskin*

"Price!" complain salespeople all over the country, "We are losing on price." Price should never be an issue if the value is there. In any market, there is a high-end provider, a middle provider, and a low-end provider. All the money is at the top or the bottom of the market. The top wins on margin and excellent fulfillment, the bottom wins on volume, and fulfillment can be in question. Whenever price is brought up as an objection, you need to examine not the dollars vs. dollars nature of the transaction. If their product is $800 and yours is $1,000, the difference is only $200. The law of business balance above is a great sales tool to use in your presentations, in your sales office, and in your sales literature because it is an eternal truth that can never be escaped.

You are never selling $1,000 vs. $800 dollars; what you are selling is the value and the difference of the $200. What does the buyer get for his extra $200? Insurance that the deliver, fulfillment, service, support, and every other component of the transaction works! Whenever prices are slashed, so is service. Walmart has low prices and absolutely zero service. Costco has low prices and absolutely zero service. Going into a grocery store like Whole Foods gives you premium prices and premium service. For the small premium what do you get? Organic well sourced food, staff that works in the store and knows about the products, and several specialty items provided and serviced in a great buying environment.

When your customer pays less, you need to remind him that he's giving something up for that small savings—the insurance that the product works, the service you bring, the guarantee you bring, and bringing them over the finish line so they are happy and you can have an ongoing lifetime relationship. The $800 item might be garbage and not work, might break, or there is no service. In today's economy of e-commerce, service and relationships are worth more than ever.

I have several vendors I purchase from who give me fair prices and excellent service. There is no need to grind them down because they deliver every time, and I am happy every time: if there is a problem, they fix it and the insurance that "this really works" is why your prices are a little higher.

When you can communicate the idea of "insurance" at a small premium to your buyer, they will see the value, and if they are smart, they will not run the risk of losing all their money in an inferior offering.

Dealing with Prospects More Powerful Than You

One challenge I have observed in my sales career is salespeople having difficulty selling and negotiating against prospects who are more powerful than they are. It's been proven in negotiation studies that the better of a negotiator you are, the more you will yield to someone who is proven to be more powerful than you. In other words, smart people psych themselves out against opponents who are more powerful than they are.

Here are some principles for dealing with people more powerful than you:

You cannot manipulate them—People who are more powerful than you have seen it all; in fact many of them wrote the book on manipulation to get into high places of power. If you try to do a "today only offer" or a gimmick, they will throw you out like a clown. You need to position yourself for power but also use zero tricks or manipulation and be very clear in all communications.

Shows like *Dragon's Den* and *Shark Tank* on mainstream television by Mark Burnett really showcase weaker players negotiating against exponentially stronger players. Typically you get to see these weaker players being destroyed like a gorilla would a rag doll. However, there are a few general rules to follow when selling or negotiating against more powerful players.

Use clear time frames upfront—Telling your more powerful player the exact time frames of how long the pitch is going to take and sticking to it is a sign of power; knowing all other time frames and revealing them in advance is impressive. Their time is at a mega premium; they want a two-minute pitch, five-minute pitch, or fifteen-minute pitch, no longer; they don't need more. When people are asking for my time, I say tell me in two sentences what you want. If they can't fit into my box, I throw them out.

Have all data printed and organized in written format with you for reference, but don't use it.—Nothing is more powerful than the written word. Showing up with the full plan written out in advance with statistics for reference is powerful, and while you keep it visible, do not hand it to them to peruse. Pitch them, and use the binder only if absolute necessary to prove something in due diligence. You can have your due diligence materials pre-prepared for their review. It's a nice gesture, but they have their own lawyers and accountants to check you out anyways. Some power players will do deeper checks into you than that.

Let them know how the process typically goes—Letting them know that they have seventy-two hours to decide on this offer upfront is what they want to know or that you stick to a maximum of three meetings is refreshing. Let them know how the sales process usually goes, and they will probably ask for some customization because they always get their way.

Even if they like it, they will have a token objection—No matter how much they like your offer, they are never going to say "yes" right away. They will always have a token objection to not make themselves feel too easy. This is good because it's real buyer's resistance; these people have something to lose by doing business with you.

Let them know you are not wasting their time—Let them know you are not going to waste their time upfront and explain how many minutes you need, whether it is sixty seconds, two minutes, or even five minutes, which is often adequate. If they want to know more they will ask you for more time.

Use the Ziff principle—done for you technique—Have everything prepared in advance so that all they need to do is sign. This is very powerful, and I secured my last book foreword by mailing a printed prototype of the book, along with a picture of me and the person at an event where we met, a letter with my request, and a pre-written forward of what he could say in a voice that sounded like him. He made some very minor revisions, signed the foreword, and called me to congratulate me. Because the process was easy for him and he could see the product, he said yes.

Use real scarcity, have a backup, never fake scarcity—Scarcity is huge for creating impulse to buy; however, powerful people do not respond to gimmicks, so if you have a scarce offer, you better have a backup or several real backups. When you can take an offer away from a powerful person, it makes them want it more and shows your power in return.

Be able to walk—want, don't need.—Never need the business; want the business. When I got into real estate investing, I invited two multimillionaires, a dentist, and an accountant to one of my flips. I was looking for a money relationship with all of them to fund my deals. One of them asked me in front of the other, "Why do you need us?" I replied, "I don't need you; I want your business." All four of them gasped because they weren't expecting this young kid to say he didn't need their money. I explained I wanted to expand and that I could continue the way I was, but I had larger ambitions. Over time all four of them became my sources of funding. Need and power are inverse and "needy" is a stinky cologne, never be needy.

Have a very short pitch—A sixty-second pitch is all you need, and if they like the sixty seconds, they will ask you for more time or to set a meeting. Often, they want the pitch in "I'm looking for X dollars to do Y with Z"— extremely simple—and if the idea makes sense, you can continue.

Be flexible with terms—Powerful people are used to having everything custom, and they are also used to exercising power. Either out of real needs or just sadism and wanting to exercise power, they will want some special terms that you normally don't do.

Never insult them—This is common sense, which is uncommon. **To powerful people, wasting time is worse than wasting money.** Keep your interaction to pure business and always agree with whatever they say; insults will kill your deal in a microsecond. Even if they say "You're ugly!" you can say, "Thank you, I haven't heard that one yet." You can have a laugh and then get on with the pitch.

They must win every time—Powerful people never lose at anything. They must always win, and if they ever feel like they are losing or getting the short end of the stick, they will get mad like a little boy and "take his ball home" and there will be no more ball playing because your powerful player "took the ball home" and away from you. You need to counterbalance this by putting up resistance to not let them steamroll you. They will test you with questions to see if you are honest or stupid. In business there are usually crooks and clowns—crooks are dishonest and steal, and clowns are just incompetent, and they don't like either.

Answer directly and be able to tell them what the downside is—They will ask you what's bad about your product or offer, so tell them straight up; don't sugarcoat it, and be prepared to show your weaknesses because that is a sign of strength. If they are interested, they will genuinely try to help you with mitigating your weaknesses with referrals to competent people.

Know your numbers inside and out memorized—Have every important number memorized. If you don't know your key numbers, you will be labelled as a clown and thrown out in a second. Looking into it and getting back to them may be acceptable, but you need to be sharper than that.

Be exactly on time—Not late, not early. Come at the exact minute. You can wait outside in the car early and show up right on time prepared. Early is rude; late is rude.

Have a token or gift—Have a leave behind, a book, a gift—the more personal and researched to their hot buttons and preferences the better. Give them something awesome; it goes a long way. Don't just give them some crap brochures that everyone receives; make it special.

Research them beforehand—Do your homework on them before you meet them, and at the very least Google them so you know the basics. The bigger the deal, the more research you need. Especially when it comes to investors or raising capital, you need to match your industry with the capital that is looking to invest in that industry. Typically, everyone loves real estate, but real estate guys don't love scrap metal because there is no security. Restaurant guys like restaurant deals and car guys like car deals, so get in the niche. It doesn't matter how great the opportunity is—if they're not predisposed towards it. If a restaurant guy doesn't understand a different industry he won't be interested in that other industry. Stay in the niche and sell to what you know.

Remember they are human beings and so are you—At the end of the day, they are human beings just like you. They bleed when wounded and sweat when tired, they sleep, they poop—they do everything the same as you. Warren Buffet, the world's richest investor, drinks Cherry Coke, eats a quarter pounder with cheese from McDonalds for lunch, and has Dairy Queen ice cream because he also owns shares in those companies. Buffet has been paraphrased as saying, "Being rich, my life is no different than yours, I drink the same coke, I eat the same cheeseburger; the only difference is long distance travel I do in a nicer way (private jet vs. economy class commercial)"

Set clear boundaries to show your power—Let them know that they should be able to make a decision in two meetings in advance (or whatever your process is). They appreciate this; otherwise you could get into a long tire-kicking session or a "not a priority" session. Be prepared to take the deal away and move on.

The Shortest Path Through the Sales Cycle (Without Cutting Corners) and Still Building Trust

When it comes to sales cycles, the shorter the better. If you can sell customers quicker it means more velocity of money for your business, more growth, and more market share. If you can eliminate any extra delays in the sales cycle, then do so. People are making faster and faster decisions to buy or not buy these days, especially with the advent of google and ecommerce. If you are selling insurance and you let them "go home and think about it," which means Googling your offer online and finding a cheaper broker.

Be prepared to close in one meeting instead of two. Cut three down to two and do as much cutting as you can without cutting the trust-building process.

The counter argument. In trust based industries, clients might need to "marinate" and become familiar with you and your brand. If you cut the sales process too quickly without any margination period, it can appear that you are too eager for the sale and only want their money. This is tough balance to strike between efficiency and trust.

A friend of mine used to work in jewelry sales in a jewelry store, and he would approach prospects as they walked in and would say, "Sir, can I help you?"

Inevitably, this is the kiss of death in retail sales. The answer was always "no"

Instead, my friend added a "marination" period: he would see the prospect, look at them over his shoulder, and politely say "Sir, I will be right with you." He would then disappear and go into the back for five minutes to let the customer peruse. He would then approach the customer and make a sale. The scarcity of the jewelry salesman created value. If you are selling a high trust item that the buyer must be "educated" on to buy, which is several high-ticket items these days, including finance, real estate, insurance, medical or any other high trust purchase, sending an information package or having an informational educational period before asking for the sale will create the trust necessary to close. Research how long this must be scientifically and cut it to where it has no more and no less than you need.

Now get out there and apply what you've learned!

To order a copy of *Self-Made* visit SelfMadeConfessions.com or StefanAarnio.com and visit the store for other books and products.

Dear Reader,

Thank you for taking the time to invest in yourself and read my work on professional selling: *The Close: 7 Level Selling*. Today is the first day on a journey towards a new level of success in your career!

The difference between the rich and the poor is how we use our time, and I hope you feel that studying this book has been a positive use of your time. Writing books is hard work, and books can be life-changing tools where, for a very small amount of money, you can make a big impact on your life. After all, your life in five years will be exactly the same as today, except for the books you read and the people you meet.

Reading books is good, but taking action in the real world is great! Get out there, and sell! Don't forget there are four simple steps to getting rich: 1) Get a job; any job will do 2) Master the art and science of straight commission sales 3) Start your own business 4) Sell your business or invest the cash flow and become a professional investor. The four steps are important, but you can't grow your money into lasting meaningful wealth without first learning to sell!

So get out there and sell! Sell something every day! A business isn't a business unless it sells something every day!

Success is your duty; you owe it to yourself and your family to reach your potential and becoming self-made in a way that only you can be proud of!

You have just read my book on sales, and as you know, after the presentation you must "close" and ask for the business! I will take my own advice and ask for your continued business if you enjoyed reading this book!

Here are some ways we can work together if you liked the value and ideas inside of this book:

The next steps for our relationship should you wish to continue working with me:

1. My company offers advanced classes for both individuals and companies on selling and closing and the methods outlined in this book. For more information you may call my office at 204–285–9882 or by email support@stefanaarnio.com

2. My company also offers one-on-one high performance coaching as well as accountability coaching for salespeople, sales teams, other companies, real estate investors, and other business people. If you are serious about reaching the next level of results in your life and business you may call my office at 204–285–9882 or email support@stefanaarnio.com

3. You may find value in the other books and products found on my website at StefanAarnio.com I offer entire product lines including motivational posters, journaling systems, diagnostic tests, and a wide selection of products to help you reach your full potential in your business and your life.

4. Let's connect on social media by Googling "Stefan Aarnio" followed by the various social media websites of the current day.

My accounts are typically @stefanaarnio, and I dominate all of
the relevant search engine space for my name "Stefan Aarnio"

5. If you are serious about succeeding in sales, business and life,
   don't let another day go by without calling me 204–285–9882
   or emailing me at support@stefanaarnio.com. My staff will bring
   your message straight to me. Let's work together to bring you the
   results you have always desired out of your career or team!

Eighty percent of books that are bought never get read! I com-
mend you for being a finisher, a closer, and finishing this book!
Readers are leaders and readers are earners! Let's connect and
work together in the pursuit of your highest and greatest self! I
believe in you.

Respect The Grind,

Stefan Aarnio

P.S. Visit StefanAarnio.com for more ways that we can work
together. We can do big things together!

MORE BOOKS BY
THE AUTHOR

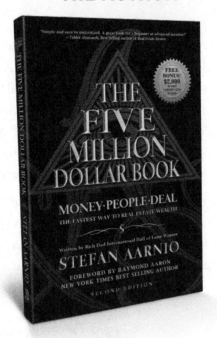

To Order, go to TheFiveMillionDollarBook.com

Stefan Aarnio is one of Canada's leading up and coming Real Estate Entrepreneurs and the winner of Canadian Real Estate Wealth Magazine's "Joint Venture Partner of the Year". Starting with only $1200, Stefan has built a multi million dollar portfolio for his partners and has earned himself a spot on The Self Made List. Stefan has accumulated properties at an alarming pace through his understanding of Real Estate Joint Ventures – The Fastest Way to Real Estate Wealth. Stefan's philosophy is simple, find great deals, build a fantastic team, pay everybody and create partnerships for life.

MORE BOOKS BY
THE AUTHOR

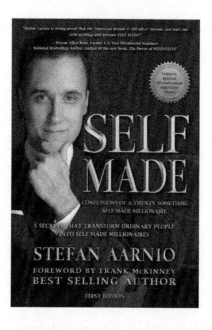

What does it take to become a self-made millionaire? Many have wondered, few have succeeded. Self Made: Confessions of a Twenty Something Self Made Millionaire follows the real life story of Stefan Aarnio, award winning real estate investor and award winning entrepreneur through the struggle of starting out with zero cash, zero credit and zero experience in his pursuit of financial freedom. Inside Self Made, you will discover the 5 Secret Skills That Transform Ordinary People Into Self Made Millionaires. These skills are mastered by the rich, purposely not taught in school and are hidden from the poor and the middle class. Join Stefan on his journey as he faces financial ruin, meets his life-changing mentor and transforms his mind, body and soul to become Self Made.

Visit **SelfMadeConfessions.com** to order and receive your bonuses!

MORE BOOKS BY THE AUTHOR

To Order visit Xnegotiation.com

What are The Ten Commandments Of Negotiation and why do we need them? Years ago in a study, 150 CEO's were contacted and were asked for the top three personality traits desired for the company's best negotiators. The top three desired traits were:

1. Personality

2. Knowledge of human nature

3. Ability to organize information

The Ten Commandments Of Negotiation are time-tested fundamentals based on these top three desired traits. If you can obey the Ten Commandments, you will be successful more times than not in any negotiation.

To Order visit Xnegotiation.com

MORE BOOKS BY THE AUTHOR

Hard times create strong men,
Strong men create good times,
Good times create weak men,
Weak men create hard times.

What does it mean to be a man?

Hard Times Create Strong Men attempts to answer the question by examining what it means to be a man in Money, Sex, Religion, and Politics using examples of what has worked throughout history.

This is not a book of feelings, in fact, you might be offended. Instead it is a book of results. What does it mean to be a man? Our current society finds that question harder and harder to answer.

The last 40% of this book is pure violence, a huge portion of the book revolves around sex, the book opens about money and finishes in the organized hate which is politics...

Parts of Hard Times will make you laugh out loud, parts will make you cry, but it is all human, real, raw and authentic and backed up by real stories from history. The arguments made are rational and based on what worked and didn't work in history to promote the survival of the tribe.

One thing is for sure, Strong Men are needed to ensure the survival of the tribe and weak men bring nothing but pain, suffering and violence outside invaders and barbarians.

Order your copy at HardTimesStrongMen.com

MORE BOOKS BY
THE AUTHOR

The High Performance Journal is the perfect complement to the Blackbook.

High performers who journal daily, write down their goals and measure their success incrementally will always outperform those who do not test and measure their success.

This journal has been designed with you in mind and is a tool for you to achieve your dreams. Big dreams are made up of small successes that slowly add up into big successes.

TheHighPerformanceJournal.com

MORE BOOKS BY THE AUTHOR

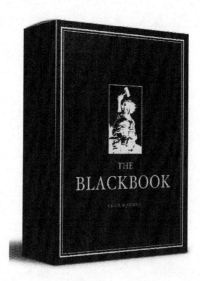

The Blackbook is the perfect complement to the High Performance Journal.

The Blackbook is designed to be a negotiation log where you can organize information you have in your dealings to win in business and in life.

TheBlackbookJournal.com

Bill Gates, Henry Ford, Oprah Winfrey, Steve Jobs and Warren Buffet all made their money in different ways. How will you make your wealth?

Find out with the Wealth Potentials personality test that measures 1) Your habits 2) Your talents and 3) Your leadership to show you how you will build your fortune and also the next steps you need to take to remove the roadblocks and reach your full potential.

How will you reach your potential for wealth?

To Find Out, visit WealthPotentials.com and take the test!

TO CA$H

Stefan Aarnio's Blueprint to cash is the
perfect "next step" for anyone curious
in learning the fundamentals of buying,
fixing and selling homes for profit!

BlueprintToCash.com

For more information on Stefan Aarnio's award winning System for finding, funding and fixing homes, please visit
TheSystemToCash.com

For a full list of products, please visit
stefanaarnio.com/store

To book speaking engagements with Stefan
please email **support@stefanaarnio.com**
or call 204-285-9882

NOTES

NOTES

NOTES

NOTES

NOTES

NOTES

NOTES

NOTES

NOTES

NOTES

NOTES

CPSIA information can be obtained
at www.ICGtesting.com
Printed in the USA
LVOW03s2048250318
571018LV00001B/2/P